"In the beginning book of the Bible, was not motivated by revenge but by love. Josh Kimbrell could have been driven by a deep resentment… but love of his son and a deep Christian faith directed him to write a powerful reflection of his personal drama and our flawed system of justice that all too often pushes Christian values out of the public arena. Josh has laid out a common sense, compassionate approach to strengthening family law."

—**The Honorable Rick Perry**, 47th Governor of Texas

"My friend, Josh Kimbrell, is one of the top conservative voices in our nation and a key Millennial leader. He is tireless in his pursuit of truth in every issue. His own story is an enlightening and cautionary tale of his own struggle for justice in a system that is well intentioned but sometimes gets it wrong."

—**Penny Young Nance**,
President, Concerned Women for America,
Fox News Contributor

"The story of Josh Kimbrell is a sad and disturbing portrayal of a father who was horribly accused of the most heinous of acts. Read the story of a man seeking justice and now a man who seeks justice for other fathers in similar circumstances."

—**Dr. Frank S. Page**, President & CEO of the
Executive Committee of the Southern Baptist Convention

"No one enjoys trials and tribulations, but we are assured in the world that we will all indeed endure them and that they actually work to mold and make us as the Lord intends. Even though we all do encounter challenges as we go through life, Josh's story of losing his son and facing public humiliation at the hands of a vengeful spouse will make you cringe and hurt for him and his son. His engaging personality and sincere heart come through in this book that tells his story but, maybe more importantly, speaks to the massive cultural problem of fatherlessness."

—**Chad Connelly**, Faith Outreach Director,
Republican National Committee

FATHERHOOD
ON TRIAL

THE FIGHT TO BE A FATHER IN
THE AGE OF DIVORCE

JOSH KIMBRELL

HIGH BRIDGE BOOKS
HOUSTON

Dedicated to all the children caught in the crossfire of
a horribly flawed family court system in our country

CONTENTS

INTRODUCTION _____ 1

PART 1: THE FATHERHOOD CRISIS IN AMERICA _____ 9

1: DISPARAGING DADS _____ 11

2: OUTLAWING FATHERHOOD _____ 19

3: DO DADS REALLY MATTER ANYWAY? _____ 33

PART 2: MY PERSONAL STORY _____ 41

4: BEGINNING MY JOURNEY TO FATHERHOOD _____ 43

5: PREGNANT AGAIN _____ 53

6: THE END OF OUR CAMELOT _____ 59

7: THE BATTLE BEGINS _____ 79

8: BLEEDING US DRY _____ 87

9: MY SON'S NEW "DADDY" _____ 99

10: A DIFFERENT STATE OF MIND _____ 107

11: ABUSING THE CRIMINAL JUSTICE SYSTEM _____ 111

12: FROM DAD TO DEFENDANT _____ 119

13: MY DAY THAT WILL LIVE IN INFAMY _____ 131

14: EXONERATION _____ 147

PART 3: THE NEED FOR FAMILY LAW REFORM IN AMERICA _ 153

15: HOW TO KEEP THIS FROM HAPPENING TO ANYONE ELSE 155

CONCLUSION: DON'T BE NEXT _____ 165

ABOUT THE AUTHOR _____ 171

INTRODUCTION

There is no experience quite as surreal or as horrifying as seeing your own mugshot flashed across the television screen during the evening news, all from the "comfort" of your very own prison cell. The horror can only be compounded by the fact that your public profile makes the news of your arrest and imprisonment a statewide story in a state in which you had long planned to run for political office. All the while, your heart breaks because you know that the charges against you—Criminal Sexual Conduct with a Minor in the First Degree, which carries a life sentence—are for allegedly molesting your own toddler child. Oh, and the accuser is your former spouse.

Sound like the makings of a *Lifetime* movie? That's what I would've said before all of this happened to me the day after Columbus Day in October of 2014.

I was born and raised in the great state of South Carolina. I grew up in the Upstate region, which is long known for its strong faith community, free market principles, and conservative politics that are as red as the clay across our foothills. For me, growing up in Upstate South Carolina was idyllic, small-town values with a world of opportunity after graduation. I loved, maybe even embodied, the culture of the state I so adored. I was baptized (twice) in middle school, graduated with honors from Chapman High School, and then completed my undergraduate studies at North Greenville University, a college that only South Carolina could create. My alma mater is a South Carolina Baptist Convention supported university where students parade around campus in Southern Tide sports shirts, sporting rainbow flip flops with Bibles in their backpacks.

In college, I was President of the Student Senate, Vice President of the Student Body, Chairman of the College Republicans, and Chairman of our South Carolina Student Legislature delegation that held a mock general assembly every year at the South Carolina State House. I interned in the South Carolina Governor's Office, worked on numerous congressional campaigns, and hosted my first public policy talk radio program on the campus station all while making the midnight IHOP runs with classmates and girls who I wanted to get to know a little better. All in all, my college experience and early adulthood were one major rush toward trying to be a voice in state politics before my 30th birthday.

Many of my friends knew I was basically nocturnal. My roommate hated that about me, but my early coffee addition and general abuse of caffeine kept me engaged with my college friends even while I worked incessantly to launch my career in the "real world." From as early as I can remember, I've been more than a little aware that death would come before I ran out of things I wanted to accomplish or dreams I wanted to come true. I don't know why I have been so exhaustingly driven since I was old enough to speak except to say that God made me this way.

Needless to say, I didn't exactly lead a normal college career or early adulthood. As a junior in college, I was encouraged by a powerful GOP strategist to run for the South Carolina House of Representatives against an incumbent that then Governor Mark Sanford wanted ousted so that school-choice legislation could move closer to law. Older and wiser friends rightly encouraged me to forego my first foray into politics at age 19, something that I resented at the time. Thus, after graduation, I took a job as a credit analyst at Carolina First Bank and founded a South Carolina public policy foundation that is now known as the Palmetto Conservative Alliance.

The drive to be the best and to be always in control of my own destiny had its costs. I ended a long-term relationship with a wonderful woman I had met as a sophomore in college so that I could more fully focus on my career. I know now that this decision was not wise and that I inadvertently hurt someone for whom I cared deeply. I probably didn't spend as much time pursuing a normal college life as much as I often think I should have. I was a man on a mission, yet I knew something was missing.

When you go to a conservative school like NGU, marriage is the major with which many of your classmates will graduate. I could not even count the number of my friends who were seriously dating or engaged by the time we walked across the stage in Turner Chapel to pick up our diplomas and receive one last famous hug from Dr. Jimmy Epting. Graduating without a significant other, even though it was my decision, gave me a slight sense of pause. I realize that many Americans now marry later in life, but being a conservative political activist in a conservative state and graduating from a conservative college probably puts a little more pressure on a person.

So, after graduation and landing my first real job while starting the policy foundation, I starting thinking about marriage and family myself. Maybe a little too much.

As I do with everything, I sat out to "solve" my singleness problem with a mighty determination. I dated more during the year and a half after I graduated than I did my entire time in college. I was determined not to fail in the area of marriage and family as surely as I was determined to succeed in business and politics. Finally, in the summer of 2008, a little over a year after graduation, I met a girl two years younger than me who was as determined to succeed in her young life as I had always been in mine. I was head over heels in no time flat.

The funny thing about meeting one's equal is that they often inspire a strange combination of instant attraction coupled with immense frustration. The very thing my then-girlfriend and I had in common—our insatiable desire to succeed—was simultaneously the source of our mutual attraction and an obstacle to our relationship. We were passionate about one another but were very determined not to allow our love for one another to short-circuit our individual desires to be the best in our respective fields.

Long story short, this young woman who I probably loved more than anyone I had ever dated to that point in my life was as driven as me, and the circumstances of our career paths ended our relationship. If the relationship had ended badly, the series of events that led to the writing of this book may well have never taken place. Messy endings tend to repel a person from immediately jumping into another romantic relationship—at least, they always have for me. Instead, the end of this relationship was as bittersweet as the entire romance had been—beautiful yet not possible. I felt like Romeo having lost Juliet and was just as love-whipped as those "star-crossed lovers."

After this wistful romance ended shortly following my 24th birthday, I felt like a man adrift. My banking career was with a company that was crumbling. I was working in a role that was more support staff than public relations and sales (which fit more closely with my personality style). My political involvement was minimal. And my personal life seemed like it was stuck in neutral.

Being the determined person that I am, I naturally doubled-down in my determination to achieve a breakthrough on all fronts. I chose to expand my policy foundation, asking experienced business and political friends of mine to join me to form a governing board of the foundation who could guide and direct it to have influence in the community and in South Carolina politics. By the time the board was formed, and I was its chairman, I was, by far, the youngest person on the panel. That was just how I wanted it; I have always believed in drawing upon the experience of those who have been high achievers with track records of success.

With my new organizational structure behind me, I set out to market my foundation and our conservative credentials around South Carolina. I started visiting Republican groups, civic organizations, churches, business events, and anywhere else I could to build our brand. This provided me with multiple speaking opportunities, which allowed me to meet many new people.

One group to which I spoke and one person who I met in early 2009 would forever alter the course of my life and career.

Even while I was trying to re-engage in politics and redirect my career, the memories of falling in love in 2008—the blissful summer I had spent with a woman I thought I would marry—continued to haunt me. I had never felt about anyone how I had felt about this person, and I was toying with the notion that I had lost my chance at a thrilling romance and the prospect of a happy marriage. The more frequently I was invited to attend—and, in some cases, be in—the weddings of my friends, the more convinced I became that I must be missing out in life.

Instead of heeding the advice of my faith as expressed in Song of Songs 8:4, "do not arouse or waken love until it so desires", I sat out to salve my soul myself. This is one area in particular where my aggressive determination did not serve me well. Anyone who has ever been in love knows that it is not formulaic. It isn't something you can manufacture or make happen. Unfortunately, the combination of my emotional vulnerability and dogged determination worked in tandem to take me down the path to grievous personal betrayal and humiliation.

My pursuit of love in the wrong place put me on a collision course that landed me on the evening news and in a Greenville County jail cell. The combination of an accusatory ex-wife, an incompetent investigator, and a politically-driven prosecutor put my precious son in foster care, my life in peril, and my career on hold. This book is the story of not only my personal trial but also a larger issue that plagues our society: the loss of fatherhood.

My story is but a microcosm, albeit an extreme one, of the larger undermining of fatherhood in our culture. The consequences could not be more severe as social ills and developmental issues abound from the lack of fatherly leadership in the lives of millions of American children. This book will outline the cultural trends toward devaluing fatherhood, which made it possible for my story to occur. It is my sincere prayer and hope that the pain my son, my family, and I endured will be used as a clarion call to change our cultural attitude toward authentic manhood and participatory fatherhood as well as to reform public policy to support two-parent childhood again.

It is my prayer that the Lord will use my story as a catalyst for the cultural and political reforms that will be required to rebuild American fatherhood and bring daddies home to their children across our country.

In the case of my nearly four-year pursuit of equal parenting time with my only son, I spent over $100,000 in legal fees, struggled to maintain any semblance of a standard of living in the process, and even went to jail so that I could spend time with my own child. No parent should have to go to prison simply for trying to be a responsible part of the lives of his or her children. I hope this book will save even one family from enduring the pain that mine and I endured for nearly five years as I fought to be a father to my beloved little boy.

PART 1

THE FATHERHOOD CRISIS IN AMERICA

CHAPTER 1

DISPARAGING DADS

"I believe that women have a capacity for understanding and compassion which man structurally does not have, does not have it because he cannot have it. He's just incapable of it."

*—**Barbara Jordan**, former Congresswoman*

"In a patriarchal society, all heterosexual intercourse is rape because women, as a group, are not strong enough to give meaningful consent."

*—**Catharine MacKinnon**, Feminist legal scholar, University of Michigan*

As a society, we have overcorrected. America has gone from Ward Cleaver to Raymond Baronne, and the result is that fatherhood is no longer respected as an honorable role to which men should aspire. In 1950s sitcoms like *Leave It to Beaver*, fathers were portrayed as epitomes of virtue who were good and noble. But by the 1990s, everybody loved Raymond, but Raymond was a moron. Dad had devolved from moral leader of his family to a hapless idiot, wandering around his own home without a clue about his children, career, or life. As a culture, we have gone from the exaggerated admiration of fathers and their spotless character to an exaggerated portrayal of men as unfeeling, unemotional, unintelligent, and immoral.

Neither extreme is healthy for family development or societal stability.

As early as elementary school, the tearing down of dad was written into children's books and story rhymes. Even the famed series, *The Bernstein Bears*, portrayed Mama Bear as loving, intelligent, and capable while depicting Papa Bear as a bumbling fool unable to look after his family. In virtually every installment of the series, which I loved as a kid, Mama Bear berated Papa Bear for being a dunce. This has made a subtle yet profound effect on the way children view the role of a father.

Take these subtleties in various book series, couple them with the generalized pop-culture portrayal of dads, and it's no wonder that we have developed a culture in our country where dads are no longer viewed as needed or respected. This has contributed to a masculinity crisis in which too many men have chosen the easy way out and abandoned the traditional roles of husband and father that are so crucial to a strong society.

Children need two parents. Nearly every study conducted on the psychology of children in various family structures has concluded that little boys and little girls are happier, healthier, and higher achievers when they have an active mother and father in their lives. It has become somehow politically incorrect to state this in our society, but it should not be considered a criticism of the millions of single moms and dads who are doing their best for their children. It is simply a statement of fact that the ideal to which we, as a society, should strive with regard to childrearing should involve an active mother and father participating in the lives of their children and engaging with them as they develop. Increasingly, this ideal is being less and less realized in America as over half of American children will spend a considerable portion of their childhood without the presence of one of their parents—usually, their fathers.

The decline of American fatherhood is absolutely related to the way our culture treats masculinity in general and fathers in particular. It's not just pop culture and sitcoms that undermine respect for fathers and fatherhood. Higher education and academia have developed entire curricula dedicated to denigrating men as barbarians who singularly aim to dominate the world in which they live, beginning with the women in their lives. As former Democratic U.S. Congresswoman Barbara Jordan once famously said,

> I believe that women have a capacity for understanding and compassion which man structurally does not have, does not have it because he cannot have it. He's just incapable of it.

With these kinds of statements and attitudes, is it any wonder that our culture has started to view dad as a dunce at best and diabolical at worst?

Fathers are now too often portrayed as necessary only for the physical function they perform that is necessary for pregnancy. In fact, famed feminist anthropologist Margaret Mead once wrote, "A father is a biological necessity but a social accident." There isn't a lot of room for misinterpretation in that statement. It is pretty clear that Mead believed that men should act as sperm donors and then leave the rearing of children and raising of families to women who have the emotional and intellectual capacity to do it more effectively. This attitude, which came to fruition in the 1960s is with us still today, and it has infiltrated our cultural, political, academic, and legal institutions and ideologies. It has undermined not only equality between men and women but also the prospect of a stable and happy childhood for millions of American children.

If the mid-20th century was a time of over-admiration of men in America, it was soon to change with the feminist movement of the 1960s led by activists like Betty Friedan. Let me be clear here that I do not believe all feminist ideas and literature are radical, extremist, or sexist concerning men. In fact, the groundbreaking book of modern feminism by Betty Friedan, *The Feminine Mystique*, released in 1963 had some legitimate points. There is no question that post-WWII America took the idea of femininity to the extreme, encouraging women to be helpless, hapless, and weak. In fact, Adlai Stevenson, a liberal Democratic politician and U.S. Ambassador, told the graduating class of the all-ladies Smith College in 1955 that they could influence America's affairs through their husbands when he said, "Women, especially educated women, have a unique opportunity to influence us, boy and man." With attitudes like that, I understand why women would feel relegated to second-class and be justifiably angry.

Feminists like Betty Friedan had no tolerance for this kind of misogyny and argued for women's equality in the workplace, in politics, and in broader American culture. Most people, the author of this book certainly included, do not view women's equality as extreme or unwelcome. If Betty Friedan had taken statements like those of Adlai

Stevenson, ripped them apart, and called for women's equality of opportunity and participation, I would have agreed with *The Feminine Mystique* and the central ideas advanced therein. That was not all she did, however. She promoted an argument that women needed to advance by tearing down the nuclear family and traditional American values. While I agree that post-war American women certainly needed greater empowerment, I don't believe that men needed to be eviscerated to achieve that equality.

Freidan argued that women could only be free when marriage was destroyed, abortion was accepted as a means of birth control, and men were emasculated. In her estimation, women could only be free when abortion was legally protected as "a woman's right to choose." Men, being the fathers of the children women carried, should have no say in the decision over whether to end the pregnancy, for doing so would infringe upon a woman's sovereignty over her own body. Friedan and her contemporaries linked women's liberation with abortion on demand and the dissolution of the family, thus undermining the moral authority of their own movement to advance women's equality.

Instead of advancing women to achieve true equality, Friedan's organization, the National Organization of Women (NOW), became more associated with liberalizing America's marriage laws, leading to the advent of so-called "no fault divorce" laws and advancing the abortion agenda. Instead of leading a broad American consensus on the importance of women's equality, Friedan and many of her associates made feminism something other than just advancing women's equality. Their agenda became a leftist political agenda that conflated feminism with tearing down traditional families and the Judeo-Christian traditions of America.

The current fatherlessness crisis we have in our country is, at least in part, the result of the misdirection of the feminist movement that began in the 1960s. Had Betty Friedan, the NOW, and other like-minded individuals and organizations advanced true women's equality—namely, equal participation in politics, the workplace, current affairs, and society—I believe we would have stronger families and a stronger culture today. Instead, Friedan and her contemporaries took the low road of advancing women's rights at the expense of men and, ultimately, the children that men and women share a part in bringing into the world.

Children should not become a pawn in the battle of the sexes as men and women struggle over who will call the shots. As actress Valerie Bertinelli once stated on an afternoon TV talk show, "You have to love your children more than you hate your ex."

I believe that men and women are equal though both sexes certainly have distinguishing characteristics and traits that make each unique. As a society, we should seek to advance the interests of all people, regardless of their gender, instead of tearing down one sex in the name of advancing the other. There is no area where this approach is more needed than the arena of parenthood. Children need both parents, and tearing down either moms or dads is a disaster in the long term. If we hope to restore American fatherhood and end the fatherlessness crisis we are experiencing in our country, we must work to restore respect for fatherhood and the men who aspire to it. This must be accomplished by men and women working together to affirm the importance of fatherly involvement in more than just the conception of a child or the writing of a child-support check.

Decades of tearing down the importance of fathers in pop-culture, political debate, and academia won't be remedied overnight. These many years of social conditioning that men are morons, dads are violent and uncaring, and that children are best raised only by mothers won't be easily overcome. Nevertheless, if we want to do what is best for our children, we must restore balance and equally honor fathers and mothers. This effort to restore respect for fatherhood is not as much about men as the children that are caught in the crossfire that erupts in the aftermath of failed marriages and families. As the next chapter lays out, the sociological and psychological consequences for America's children should rouse us to action on this issue before more children are forced to endure single-parent childhood.

CHAPTER 2

OUTLAWING FATHERHOOD

The cultural assault on the role of a father has gone far beyond a few negative sitcoms or tirades by college professors and members of Congress. For the past half century, we have witnessed the legal undermining of fatherhood, which has frozen many fathers out of the lives of their children once their marriage or relationship falls apart. One of the major driving factors in the epidemic of fatherlessness we are experiencing in this country is that family courts regularly relegate one parent, usually the father, to nothing more than an occasional visitor to their children. In my home state of South Carolina, our family-court system almost always follows "Judge Brown's Rules" with regard to non-custodial parental visitation. Because about 90% of non-custodial parents are fathers, these rules almost always apply to the dad. They basically make the father financially responsible for the rearing of their children but not vested with any decision-making authority or significant presence with their children.

Judge Brown's Rules and the similar guidelines enacted in most states in the Union typically allow non-custodial parents to visit their children on only four days per month and one night per week for several hours, which works out to less than 20% of any given year. With fathers seeing their children less than 20% of the time on average, is it any wonder that their children exhibit social and developmental issues that arise from the absence of a two-parent home? The best scientific and sociological evidence has concluded that children begin developing strong biological attachment to their parents as early as two months old, which means that a child taken from his or her parents before that period of time or after is robbed of the critical opportunity to bond with one parent. This is an incredibly traumatic event in the lives of young children.

In my case, my former wife elected to leave our marriage when our son was four weeks old. He was on the cusp of developing these critical attachments to me as his father when he was ripped from my life for nearly a year before I could reestablish any sort of relationship with him. To this day, he still has separation anxiety issues, and I have much more time with him than most fathers would ever dream of having with their children post-divorce. This sort of scenario has been replicated over and over in every state in the nation with millions of children being consigned to a government-mandated, single-parent childhood.

The legal assault on American fatherhood began in earnest at roughly the same time when activists like Betty Friedan declared that the nuclear family was a "comfortable concentration camp" for women. The organization that Friedan founded, the National Organization for Women (NOW), remains the largest and most powerful feminist organization in America, and it is wholly dedicated to left-wing political causes as discussed in the prior chapter. The NOW has taken the position that women are the primary caregivers of children and that, increasingly, fatherly involvement in the lives of children is not necessary for childhood stability. Such a statement defies an entire body of research on child developmental psychology that reaches the exact opposite conclusion. In spite of all the evidence, organizations like NOW continue to peddle the myth that two-parent childrearing is not healthier for children.

Moral feminism should be concerned with ensuring equality and equal opportunity for women, not attempting to tear down men. When Betty Friedan wrote *The Feminine Mystique,* there was certainly a need for women's advocacy to ensure that women had equal access to higher education, the boardroom, and political positions. Instead of addressing these issues and attempting to provide equal opportunity to women, activists like Betty Friedan bought into the notion that women could only be advanced if men were demeaned. As such, feminist activists began seeking family law reforms that would make it easier to end the "concentration camp" without cashing-out of the income stream. "No-fault divorce" laws made it easier for women to apply for alimony and child support even if they chose to leave their husbands for no other reason than that they wanted to try something new.

There is no doubt that women in 1963 had less access to well-paying jobs to support themselves in the event that their marriages dissolved or they never married in the first place, something that rightly needed to be remedied. But the NOW and other such organizations saw an opportunity for revenge. Instead of advocating for alimony and child support in instances wherein men committed adultery or were demonstrably abusive, many feminist organizations began arguing for such financial support from former husbands and fathers even if no such condition existed—even if the man did not abandon or abuse his family or act unfaithfully to his spouse. There was certainly a critical need to improve women's access to the economy and to ensure that she wasn't viewed as subservient to her husband in family-court cases. However, what NOW and its affiliates did was to overcorrect by making men sub-servient in family-court cases. This has resulted in men being treated like financial resources and visitors to their children—not as equal parents.

In short, many left-leaning feminists have abandoned the noble idea of women's equality and have instead engaged in reshaping family law to ensure that women almost always obtain primary custody of children while fathers receive the primary financial responsibility to support the child. Thus, instead of advocating for equality of the sexes, such an agenda actually seeks to put men at a considerable disadvantage in the legal system with regard to divorce and custody cases. For decades, family courts have prevented millions of men from being active participants in the lives of their children while ordering them to pay the overwhelming majority of the costs associated with raising the child they rarely see.

Family court has become the radical Left's greatest tool of social reengineering. Instead of two parents making decisions about how to raise their own children, family courts freeze out fathers and empower not only mothers but unaccountable judges who make absolute decisions without the presence of a jury or, in many cases, the opportunity for appeal. Family courts influence a child's standard of living, educational arrangements, and even religious instruction.

In 2009, a Chicago circuit court judge issued a restraining order against a man named Joseph Reyes that prohibited Mr. Reyes from taking his then three-year-old daughter to any non-Jewish religious event because to do so would "contribute to the emotional detriment of the child." The reason this order was issued was that the little girl's mother, Mr. Reyes's former partner, is Jewish and wanted her daughter to be raised according to her own religious tradition. As such, the State of

Illinois ordered the child's father not to take his own daughter to an event associated with the Christian, or any other, religious tradition because it was not in keeping with the religious preferences of the mother.

During my over four-year custody battle, I was ordered to use my former wife's preferences for our son's medical care, dietary program, and educational instruction. While my opinion about raising our son did not matter, I was still ordered to pay full medical insurance costs, medical co-pays, and over $700 additional dollars in child support to my son's mother even though she left our marriage and refused to reconcile. Thus, at a time when I had little to no interaction with my son, I was forced to pay all costs or face jail time while simultaneously having to finance my own legal struggle to be a parent to my own child.

I am not a father who would ever complain about financially providing for my own child. I believe that any man who has a child has a moral obligation to seek to provide for that child. I do not believe, however, that his manner of financially supporting his child should be mandated by a court under penalty of prosecution when he is seeking to provide for and be active in the life of his child. However, this is not the position of activist family courts who have so financially burdened many men who are still fighting to be active parents that they simply cannot afford to pay attorneys to remain in their child's life.

One of the most egregious child support cases in recent history took place in Georgia in 2009. A man named Frank Hatley was imprisoned for more than a year because of his failure to pay back child support payments for a child who was not biologically his own. A court order signed in 2001 when he and his ex-girlfriend split up acknowledged that DNA testing had confirmed that he was not the biological father of his girlfriend's daughter but still held him responsible for financial support of her child due to the longevity of their relationship. Mr. Hatley, who did not make a great deal of money, went about working numerous jobs to comply with the court order on child support, even being forced to live in his own car so that he could afford to pay the court. Despite all the sacrifices, he still fell behind in support and was held in contempt of court for failure to pay.

After a year in jail, a public defender was able to secure Mr. Hatley's release from prison and to end any future child support payments to his ex-girlfriend for the child who was not his. However, he was not released from his obligation to pay over $250 per month until the $16,000 in back child support was paid in full. While this is an extreme example, it underscores the financial and personal pain many fathers—or, in the case of Mr. Hatley, temporary stepfathers—feel when they encounter our nation's broken family-court systems. The costs associated with fighting for any semblance of custody while also having to pay exacting child support to their former partners leave many men financially broke and without any role in their child's life. Such personal and financial pain has led many fathers to give up the fight to be an active parent to their children—sometimes, they resort even to alcoholism and suicide.

Our state family-court systems are in dire need of reform and not just for the sake of desperate fathers. Millions of children are being deprived of caring parents—and, by extension, grandparents, aunts, and uncles—because family courts force one parent out of the picture. This is an issue that affects both men and women and is a cultural imperative. Yet, when disenfranchised fathers so much as suggest that family law be reformed, they are often attacked as anti-mother, misogynist, or are outright defamed. I have personally experienced these accusations, so I can speak about them firsthand.

In 2012, less than one year after my former wife left our home with our son, I had already concluded that the family court would be one of my biggest obstacles to being involved in his young life. After having already spent thousands of dollars in legal costs, I was still seeing my son only hours per week and had absolutely no overnight visits because my former wife had, without any evidence, accused me of not feeding our child and of trying to boil him in hot water. The Greenville County South Carolina Family Court sided with my former wife even though she could not substantiate her unfounded claims, and I was frozen out of my son's life for over a year.

When word reached me that a group of concerned citizens were going to lobby the South Carolina Legislature for family law reform in the 2012 legislative session, I was interested in engaging. Through my daily primetime radio program and its corresponding policy foundation, I thought I may be able to add a personal perspective and public pressure to these efforts to update outdated laws. Little did I know just how vicious this debate would become from the start of the debate. I was unaware of just how entrenched certain special interest groups had become on this issue, and they were prepared to unleash with all of their fury.

The most vicious opponents of our common-sense, shared-parenting proposals were the people who prosper most from the current dysfunction: family law attorneys. They teamed up with activists from the National Abortion Rights Action League (NARAL) and the National Organization for Women (NOW) to defeat each of our legislative proposals. Their strategy was to portray any and all fathers who advocated for equal parenting reforms as former abusers and child molesters who were just a bunch of sour grapes.

I remember a particularly nasty series of South Carolina Senate subcommittee hearings on shared parenting in which I participated. The senate judiciary committee had established a bipartisan subcommittee to hear arguments on family law reform, which turned out to be one of the most contested committee hearings of the 2012 legislative session. I was helping to lead a coalition of family-law reform advocates who felt that our custody laws were particularly unfair to children who were legally deprived of having a relationship with both of their parents. Those of us advocating for reform were a diverse bunch, ranging from a pharmacist to social workers, who wanted to see shared parenting become a reality in South Carolina.

Our policy analysts had put together companion legislative proposals to be considered in both the State House and the State Senate simultaneously. The proposals were not radical; they were adopted from similar reforms enacted in the states of Minnesota and Maryland that changed family-court guidelines to provide for shared parenting absent clear evidence of abuse, neglect, or abandonment. The central and most-contested element of our reform package was a change to the custody guidelines that family-court judges must adhere to when making custody decisions in family court during divorce and separation proceedings. Our proposal was that there should be a *presumption* (a legal term meaning "expected unless circumstances warranted otherwise") of joint custody with equal visitation and shared decision-making power for both mothers and fathers unless one party had committed adultery and abandoned their family, had abused one's spouse and/or children, or had a record of drug abuse or alcoholism.

Even with all of these caveats included in our proposal, it was immediately ridiculed by the South Carolina Bar Association as radical and unworkable. In fact, the Bar unleashed the head of their family law division—an attorney who actually specialized in a procedure known as *judicial bypass*, which helps underage girls obtain abortions without parental notification—to tear down our proposal's credibility which she did by attacking us personally. Her name was Pat Forbis, and she testified to the State Senate on the same day that I did.

On the morning I rose to speak, I made the case that too many children in South Carolina were being deprived of a two-parent childhood because of overactive family courts operating on outdated family law statutes. I told the senators that so-called *temporary hearings*—which are initial 15-minute custody hearings when a couple separates that set "temporary" custody and financial guidelines—are too often ambushes in which parents seek to go nuclear, legally speaking, on their former partner. The reason former spouses go all in on temporary hearings is that, more often than not, these temporary hearings set the stage for the final custody order when the divorce and/or custody case is finalized even though they are said to be "without prejudice."

The combination of 80%-20% custody arrangements—which is the norm in most states in America in which one parent will get 80% of the time and primary legal custody while the other gets 20% visitation and no decision-making authority—and a 15-minute hearing that will make that determination makes two people who already don't like one another totally hate one another. It was under these circumstances that my former wife would begin hurling accusations at me that would, eventually, result in my being falsely arrested, imprisoned, and publicly humiliated.

I was blindsided by my wife's leaving our marriage less than a month after our son was born, and I desperately wanted to figure out what went wrong and reunite our family. As such, I didn't "lawyer up" right after she left with our infant son. Following the advice of marriage counselors and clergy from our church, I tried to deescalate the situation and did not aggressively assert my parental rights. For months, I saw our son only in a Greenville coffee shop near my wife's parents with her entire family sitting there watching me interact with my son from whom I had been prematurely separated. After all of my pleas for reconciliation, to go to marriage counseling, and to work this out on our own, my wife had me served with separation and divorce papers at my home. The temporary hearing was set, and it was time for me to retain counsel.

The first temporary hearing was, as I've described already, war. My wife's attorney came in armed with a litany of lies to try and bury me from the very outset of the separation and divorce proceedings. In those 15 minutes before a Greenville County Family Court judge, my wife's attorney accused me of being mentally unfit to be a parent, trying to starve our son, burning him on the stove top, boiling him in a pot of hot water, trying to break his neck, and the list goes on. None of these things were true, and there were no police call records. No evidence. Nothing. But that didn't matter. I was the father, and I was already at a disadvantage for that reason alone. The court awarded my wife sole "temporary custody" and ordered that I see my son only with supervision.

This judgement made at this temporary hearing took effect almost immediately with me being ordered to pay not only all of my son's expenses but for my wife's car, her cellphone bill, and her health insurance (in addition to our son's). The judge also ruled that I could only see him twice a month with parental supervision. This was just humiliating. In a matter of months, my wife left me, my son was taken from me, and I was treated by the family court as a violent abuser with absolutely no evidence that this was ever the case. The family court was my wife's greatest ally in forcing me out of my child's life.

These were the experiences that motivated me to use my radio and public policy platform to try and move the needle with regard to family law reform in my state. It was pretty clear to me that the way I was treated was not an isolated incident but, instead, part of a more prevalent pattern of family courts taking children from one parent—normally, the father—while granting nearly everything to the other. It was a system that rewarded lies and fabrications and didn't place much of a premium on accuracy with regard to accusations. This sort of bankrupt system that ripped children from their fathers, financially punished one parent for no other reason than that their relationship had ended, and forced children into a government-mandated, single-parent childhood could not stand. Something needed to be done.

Family law has been abused by leftist organizations intent on social engineering for decades. Not only have certain radical feminist groups— not to be confused with legitimate women's advocacy groups that care about women's equality rather than emasculating men, wonderful organizations like Concerned Women for America—tried to use family law to subjugate men and force them from their children's lives, but Marxist organizations that seek to socialize American society have sought to impose state involvement in family life. Family law has become so expansive that family courts have issued orders to parents regarding their children's religious instruction, dietary requirements, schooling arrangements, and even clothing choices. There is no role for government to make decisions for children that are rightly the prerogative of parents—both parents.

Family law reform is critical for the future of America's children for two primary reasons. First, children need both parents, something that most states' current family law codes do not provide for. Second, both parents should have priority when it comes to making decisions for their children—not government bureaucrats and judges in black robes. Family law reform, which we will discuss in the closing chapter of this book, is necessary for securing the futures of millions of children across this country. It is equally about solidifying equal parental rights for mothers and fathers and about securing the rights of both parents against the encroachment of an ever-expanding governmental involvement.

Entrenched special interests—particularly, state bar associations— that have a vested financial interest in the current system of chaos will oppose reform at every juncture, and they will demonize anyone who disagrees with them. If we are ever to achieve victory for our children, we must find the courage to resist such bullying by those with vested financial interests that continually pit mothers' and fathers' advocacy groups against one another just as the courts pit mothers and fathers against one another in family court. Mothers and fathers may disagree with one another's parenting styles, and they may absolutely despise one another by the time the divorce proceedings come, but they must collectively resist government tyranny that tramples their rights as parents to make responsible decisions for the children that they love.

For decades, family law has been used by radical feminist organizations to undermine the rights of fathers. But now, the issue has expanded. Parenthood as a whole is in real danger of being ceded to the preeminence of the courts, and this is a danger to both parents and, above all, to the children that they share. Shared parenting is the right thing to do for both parents, for children, and for the cause of free and limited government in our country.

CHAPTER 3

DO DADS REALLY MATTER ANYWAY?

"A father is a biological necessity but a social accident."

–Margaret Mead, Feminist Anthropologist

There are some folks in academia, pop culture, and politics—as we discussed in the first chapter—who believe that the entire concept of fatherhood is overblown. They argue that fathers essentially perform only a biological function and little else. As famed feminist anthropologist Margaret Mead, a contemporary of NOW founder Betty Friedan, once said, "A father is a biological necessity but a social accident." The idea that men have nothing to offer children is not a sentiment that is shared by most people in this country, including the overwhelming majority of women in America. It is, however, a belief shared by too many liberal elites who have incredible influence over media and entertainment, politics and public policy, and higher education and academia. As we've discussed in the previous two chapters, there has been a concerted effort on multiple fronts to undermine the importance of fathers and their roles in family life.

Liberal elites have sought for decades to undermine the nuclear family as doing so makes it much easier for government to play a more prominent role in the rearing of the next generation. The nuclear family, as Aristotle argued, is the "well-ordered society in seed form." The first experience most of us have with authority, government, civil structure, religious values, economic principles, and moral development occurs within the confines of our families. As such, there can be no more critical structure of society than strong families. With America's divorce rate hovering at around 55% for first marriages, 67% for second marriages, and 73% for third marriages, it's no secret that the family is under fire. Take this trend, and add to it the constant undermining of one of a child's two parents after separation/divorce—normally, the father—and we have a recipe for national cultural chaos.

The past 50 years in America have been an incredible sociological case study. As the family has fallen further from national favor and two-parent homes have become increasingly hard to come by, sociological ills from mass murders to rape and drug abuse have risen rampantly. There is a sociological connection between children being raised without a strong family structure and social adjustment issues as well as criminal behavior in adolescence and adulthood. These social ills have led to an increase in the size and scope of government as government programs have tried unsuccessfully to fill the void left by failed families.

There is no question that much of this pressure on the family has been brought to bear by the devaluation of dads. I have always believed in the equality of men and women and will always believe in it. Equality does not negate uniqueness, however, and there are very specific sets of skills and values instilled in children by both mothers and fathers. Fathers also have a unique role of leadership within the nuclear family, something that God established for the good of the family structure He ordained. Leadership does not mean dictatorship, however, and men are not superior to women just because they are called to lead their families. As discussed in the first chapter, certain radical feminist organizations promote the idea that male leadership of the home amounts to a "comfortable concentration camp" for women and seek to overthrow men from leading their families. This has been done to the detriment of men, women, and, especially, children.

Single-parent homes, often headed by single mothers, are 50% more likely to live at or below the poverty line, and children raised in those homes are more likely to be economically disadvantaged as adults themselves. Single mothers, and the much-smaller number of single dads, often struggle to balance the rigorous demands of single parenthood while also working to maintain their jobs and the household they now head alone. Two-parent homes simply function best as mothers and fathers can mutually reinforce one another and help one another balance the demands of daily living. Our divorce and single-parenthood culture has weakened the fabric of our society and grown government into our partner in raising our children. This has come with a loss of autonomy and liberty, which is the tradeoff for government-provided economic security.

Even if we cannot improve the divorce rate in the near term, we can take meaningful steps to ensure that both parents maintain a presence and role in their children's lives in the aftermath of failed families. This will soften the economic, psychological, and emotional blow to children and parents that accompanies separation and divorce. In order to achieve this meaningful reform, we will have to convince our fellow citizens of the importance of fathers as they have been the overlooked parent for far too long. We must affirm the importance of both parents and encourage mothers and fathers alike to fulfill their responsibilities to their children regardless of their relational or marital status.

Belief in the importance of fathers is a bipartisan conviction. The left-leaning Brookings Institute published an excellent piece in the summer of 2014 that was written by Senior Fellow for Economic Studies Isabel V. Sawhill in which she asserted that "children raised by single mothers are more likely to fare far worse on a number of dimensions, including their school achievement, their social and emotional development, their health and their success in the labor market." Ms. Sawhill, who served as a deputy director of the Office of Management and Budget (OMB) during the Clinton Administration, went on to assert that "they are at greater risk of parent abuse and neglect (especially from live-in boyfriends who are not their biological fathers), more likely to become teen parents and less likely to graduate from high school or college." I would say that it is fair to conclude that this former Clinton Administration official has determined that dads do matter, and it is time more leaders in our culture reach these same conclusions.

Whole hosts of social statistics make the case for fatherhood stronger than any words I can write. The U.S. Census Bureau's "Children's Living Arrangements and Characteristics" data tables from 2011, echoing the words of Ms. Sawhill from the Brookings Institute, indicates that children in fatherless homes are almost four times more likely to be poor. The research showed that 12% of children in two-parent homes lived in poverty while over 44% of children in fatherless homes lived at or below the poverty line. In a 1993 publication on alcohol and drug abuse, the U.S. Department of Health and Human Services stated that "fatherless children are at a dramatically greater risk of drug and alcohol abuse." A May 2012 article in *Psychology Today* written by Dr. Edward Kruk, "The Vital Importance of Paternal Presence in Children's Lives", indicated that over 71% of high-school dropouts in America come from fatherless homes, a statistic that bolsters the Brookings Institute's conclusions that children without active fathers do not perform as well academically.

The sad trail of evidence continues into other serious crime statistics as over 80% of men who commit and are convicted of rape crimes come from homes where no father was present. Similarly sad statistics are true for burglary, domestic abuse, and murder. A generation of fatherless men are wandering America's streets, looking for purpose, meaning, and role models. Unfortunately, the hunger for male affection and discipline is creating a cultural crisis that is adversely affecting everyone in America.

This phenomenon is not unique to America. A 2011 study completed by the Melbourne Institute of Applied Economic and Social Research at the University of Melbourne (Australia) stated that "the sense of security generated by the presence of a male role model in a youth's life has protective effects for a child, regardless of the degree of interaction between the child and father." The report goes on to determine that "fathers provide children with male role models and can influence children's preferences, values and attitudes, while giving them a sense of security and boosting their self-esteem. They also increase the degree of adult supervision at home, which may lead to a direct reduction of delinquent behavior."

With such a body of evidence as the importance of involved fathers in their children's lives, it is truly amazing that so many in our society continue to downplay the importance of fatherly involvement with their children.

Mothers and fathers bring unique characteristics to children's lives that are critical to their wellbeing. Mothers are, by nature, more inclined to be nurturing to children (not to suggest that dads aren't nurturing as well, but moms are primal nurturers) and are more likely to discuss feelings and emotions with their children. At the same time, fathers are primal hunter-gatherer types who teach their children logic skills and how to deal with life when it knocks them down. While mothers and fathers each specialize in certain skill sets, those skills are not exclusive to one sex. In other words, while mothers are more inclined to be nurturing, it doesn't mean that dads cannot be nurturing. I adore my son, and I cuddle, hold, and kiss him on the cheek every chance I get. While fathers are more naturally inclined toward logic and methodical problem solving, this does not mean that women are illogical or unable to provide (i.e. be "hunter-gatherers").

Our culture needs to stop with the battle of the sexes when it comes to which parent is best. The answer is that neither parent is best and that we're better together. This does not necessarily mean that we're better together in the sense that moms and dads must stay married although I do believe that is ideal. It means that both parents should stay with their children and be equally involved with them, regardless of the parents' relationship with one another. Despite the importance of both parents to childhood development, a quick Google search on the internet will yield thousands of results with titles similar to "Why Mothers Make Better Parents than Fathers" and "Why Mom's Bond with the Children is More Important." There is no shortage of this sort of literature out there, and it is not productive to understanding the mutual importance of mothers and fathers.

I know too many men who have given up the fight to be a father. After my story became public in the aftermath of my arrest for false allegations that I will detail in later chapters, I received literally thousands of messages from across South Carolina from fathers, mothers of those fathers, and second wives who shared with me horror stories about how the man in their lives was forced from being involved with his own children because of outdated family court laws and a cultural bias against the importance of fathers. Being a father after divorce is an uphill battle, one that usually costs many thousands of dollars, years of emotional turmoil, and dozens of court appearances and legal battles. In the face of such daunting odds, many men just checkout and sign over their children because they simply cannot afford to fight any longer… neither financially nor emotionally.

I can relate. After my marriage fell apart in the summer of 2011, I was embroiled in a custody/legal battle that, ultimately, landed me in jail in the fall of 2014 and still in family law litigation at the time of this writing. I have personally spent nearly $100,000 over the past nearly five years and have struggled financially, emotionally, and even publicly all because I refused to quit on my little boy. I have, like many men, entertained the idea of giving up and giving in because the costs involved in continuing the battle are so horrendous. All that has kept me going is the sweet words, "Daddy, I love you," and the sweet kiss on the cheek from an innocent little boy who does not deserve to be abandoned by his dad.

The importance of a father in the lives of his children cannot easily be overstated. Both parents are precious and irreplaceable to a child and to his or her healthy development. Steps must be taken to ensure that dads have a fighting chance to stay involved in the lives of their children, just as much as that opportunity should be afforded to mothers. The evidence is indisputable: two-parent homes are the ideal setting for chil-drearing and, in the absence of a nuclear, two-family home, the next best option is two active parents who put their child's interests ahead of their own personal animosities.

PART 2

MY PERSONAL STORY

CHAPTER 4

BEGINNING MY JOURNEY TO FATHERHOOD

I met my first wife at an emotionally vulnerable moment in my life and in the most unusual of circumstances. Following the end of my relationship with a woman I thought I might marry, I was in search of a way to salve my wounds. As has typically been my default, I threw myself fully back into my work, hoping that pursuing career goals would gloss over the sense of sadness that I felt. I doubled-down on promoting my policy foundation and engaging in public policy issues that I cared about.

As I normally did in college, my intention was to shift my attention back to my work and away from personal pursuits. I thought I would drown my personal-life goals in a sea of setting goals and fighting to achieve them. Little did I know that I would soon see an outlet for my pent up desire for a family life at a speaking event that was part of my grand strategy of distracting myself from those pursuits.

It was March of 2009 when I walked into a dinner meeting of the Upstate Young Republicans at Mythos family restaurant in Greer, South Carolina to pitch my new policy foundation. A local business owner, a friend of mine, was there to announce that he was running for the U.S.

Congress from the Fourth District, and I was there to try and gain some volunteers for my foundation's legislative efforts. The crowd was large and young, something that excited conservative activists in the aftermath of our party's drubbing in the presidential race the fall prior.

It was more than just the crowd that had my attention, however, and my mind started racing.

A stunningly beautiful, even if slightly punky, young woman was nestled among the tightly-packed crowd, brimming with energy and enthusiasm. She was talkative and engaging but not your typical Young Republicans activist. Maybe it was her uniqueness that held such appeal to me, but one thing was certain in my mind: I needed to get to know this girl a little better. I made it a point to invite her to coffee… to discuss political ideas, of course.

To my surprise, she readily agreed to meet me the following week at a Greenville-area Starbucks to, as far as she knew, discuss the meeting where we had met and my ideas for engaging South Carolina politics. I had little interest in discussing politics with her; I was much more interested in the personal details. However mature I may or may not have been at age 24, I still completely engaged in the "boy-meets-girl" goofiness that makes romance such an exciting, if sometimes excruciating, experience.

At that first coffee meeting, I showed up wearing South Carolina Palmetto Tree sandals, jeans, and a polo with nothing but a cellphone in my hands. She came with a notepad and pencil ready to conduct a full-blown business meeting. After grabbing a couple of coffees, I think I managed to convince her that I wasn't really all that interested in a business meeting. We started talking about our likes and dislikes, childhood years, and favorite things. One thing that stuck out to me in that early meeting was how, despite our different styles and circumstances, our lives and interests seemed so similar.

Over the next several months, I plowed ahead deeper and deeper in love with a woman I thought I knew but feared that I didn't. Nevertheless, the spontaneity of the relationship and the joy of camaraderie kept my attention and kept me on the road to marriage. Cassidy was a very physical person as am I, so the real fireworks of the relationship were the physical aspects. It quickly became obvious that we were moving rapidly down the relationship rollercoaster, and I wanted to be sure that we did things the right way. I certainly didn't want to put us in the position where we might be parents before we were married—before we were sure we would stay together—because I had heard horror stories from too many friends who grew up torn between two parents.

I was determined to do things right with Cassidy for our sake and for the sake of any family we might ever have together. It was important to me to marry this woman whom I loved and to start a life together. Though I did have some concerns about Cassidy, I felt they were probably just the result of my trepidation about commitment, a byproduct of my excessive focus on career and calling that I had throughout my college years. I was determined to let down my guard and trust someone. I threw caution to the wind and was determined to give myself to the woman who I had quickly decided that I loved.

As such, I asked Cassidy to marry me in the late summer of 2009 on the campus of my alma mater, North Greenville University, after we drove up there for coffee one evening. I hit one knee in front of the main fountain at the entrance of the campus, just as a light rain was beginning to fall. The moment was pretty special and exhilarating. I always assumed I would marry, but graduating and starting my career without a family or even a serious girlfriend had pushed that from my mind. Rising to my feet with a ring on Cassidy's finger felt right. It was the start of family life, and I was brimming with excitement about our future together.

I was the happiest man in the world. I was getting married and would be starting a family of my own. I got a promotion at Carolina First Bank just after the engagement was announced. My career, my emerging family, and everything else seemed to be coming together for me by the fall of 2009. I thought the fall of 2009 was the happiest time of my life and that the road ahead was paved with promise and unending happiness.

We were wed in a small chapel off the main sanctuary of Taylors First Baptist Church, just outside Greenville, South Carolina on October 24, 2009 by my friend, Dr. Frank S. Page. That October day was amazing. It was an unusually warm October day in the Upstate, and there was hardly a cloud in the sky; it was stunning. Nothing about the weather or my day indicated the coming storm that was about to be unleashed with all its fury. As far as I was concerned, that October day was the beginning of the rest of my life with a woman whom I deeply loved and adored. I still to this day remember by heart the reply of Ruth from the Old Testament that we were led to recite during our ceremony: "I will neither leave you nor turn back from you. Where you go I will go, and where you stay I will stay. Your people will be my people and your God my God."

I meant it. I had prayed like never before in my life going into that chapel, and I was determined not to mess my marriage up. I had mentally overcome my objections and was ready to build a life with this woman who I didn't even know a year ago. Ours had been a whirlwind relationship; it had only been eight months from the time we met to the time we married. I made the most monumental commitment of my early life in less time than it had taken me to officially pick colleges after high school!

On my wedding day, though, none of that seemed to matter. I was convinced that our romance was real, and I had swayed myself to believe that all of the inconsistencies Cassidy had displayed in our short dating life were no big deal or, perhaps even more so, something that I had misunderstood. Being the political enthusiast that I am, I remembered reading the book, *George and Laura: Portrait of An American Marriage*, in a high school class. The two of them met and were married within one month, and that marriage has obviously lasted. I had many friends, young and old alike, tell me that they had a short dating/courtship period and that everything had worked out fine. By the time I said "I do", I did have confidence in my decision.

That confidence would be short lived. In fact, the turbulence in my new marriage would begin on the honeymoon though this had little to do with our personalities. The swine flu had been sweeping through much of the country in the fall of 2009 with record numbers of people experiencing a very intense bout of flu symptoms that included high fever, body aches, and nausea. This type of flu wasn't really covered by the flu shot, which contributed to its virulence. Little did Cassidy and I know that we were already getting sick at the time we took our wedding vows.

When we left our wedding reception, we were starving. We had decided to spend most of our time talking to our guests, and the food was largely gone by the time we ever got around to eating. Not wanting to starve before we arrived for our honeymoon in Sevierville, Tennessee, we stopped by Chick-Fil-A still in our wedding clothes and with "JUST MARRIED" scribbled across our back window. I am sure we were an entertaining sight for the folks working the drive through that day.

The drive to Tennessee was incredible. We ate our Chick-Fil-A nuggets, laughed and rejoiced about the day that had just passed, and anticipated our first night together as a married couple. The first night and the next day were fantastic, and it seemed as if our unlikely romance was working out better than anybody had anticipated, including me.

The first full day of our honeymoon was thrilling and playful. We went to a breakfast restaurant downtown and then to Dollywood to ride the rollercoasters and the 110 coal-powered steam locomotive that the park has maintained and operated since I was a little boy. The warmth of the wedding day had started to give way to the more seasonal crispness of the late-October day. That made cuddling on the open-air locomotive moving through the mountain even more romantic.

After we finished freezing in the park, we decided to go grab pizzas at a local mountain pizzeria that we could take back to our cabin for an evening in the hot tub. Before we ever made it back to the cabin, I felt the fever starting to grip me. The fever was just the beginning. On the short drive from the theme park to our mountain cabin (after a stop to pick up pizza), the body aches began… the chills… the whole enchilada. My new wife was very understanding and caring, which gave me more encouragement about the decision we had made to get married; however, being horribly ill on a trip that was supposed to be filled with fun, lovemaking, and laying the foundation for a family wasn't all that reassuring. It was certainly a rough way to start.

My symptoms only lasted for about 24 hours, so by the time we left Tennessee, I was feeling fine again. Cassidy, however, had the same symptoms that had hit me at the end of our first full day of our honeymoon. So, as we started home, I was nursing the sick wife who had nursed me back to health just a day ago. While our honeymoon didn't exactly go as planned or expected, we still had a sense of optimism as we headed home to Columbia finally to setup life together.

Moving home would be the first time I would notice that something was amiss with our relationship. It seemed that we had more than disagreements. We had totally different worldviews that would cause tension in our marriage from the outset.

While I have always wanted children, the start of our marriage was rocky and unstable. I thought that having children should come later, something on which Cassidy and I seemed to agree. When I expressed my concerns to Cassidy, however, she indicated that she had some issues that would make it nearly impossible for her to get pregnant. In other words, she assured me that, even without the use of any sort of birth control, she wasn't sure she would be able to get pregnant. This gave me a mix of emotions: short-term comfort that we wouldn't easily become pregnant and have children until we were more settled but also the overriding concern that we may never be able to have children together. All of this seemed so strange to me because Cassidy's story on these things seemed to evolve. This was never something she had shared with me while we were dating or even after we were married until it became an immediate issue.

We learned that we were pregnant in early March of 2010. When we found out, it was pretty obvious that Cassidy wasn't very far along; we even joked that it must have happened on Valentine's Day. I was pretty much in shock when she first told me, but it was a mixture of fear and excitement. I had always wanted to be a daddy, but I certainly wasn't planning on it happening within the first year of being married. Instead of dwelling on not being prepared to be a parent, I wanted to support and encourage Cassidy and to express the excitement we both felt. My colleagues at work, however, encouraged me to be careful building it up too much with our families, even with Cassidy, because we were early in the first trimester, a time notorious for miscarriages. We didn't listen and, instead, went to the Upstate together that weekend to tell our families and visit a few baby stores.

Just before we left the Upstate for the return ride to Columbia on Sunday night, March 7th, Cassidy noticed that she was spotting a little more than she thought was usual based on the information we had read. Obviously, we were concerned, but we thought it probably wasn't anything unexpected or extraordinary. We decided to go ahead and head home because I had to work on Monday morning, and we thought Cassidy may do better to rest at home. The further down the interstate we went, the more cramping Cassidy was experiencing and the more concerned we were becoming.

Neither of us was prepared for what would come next. About 45 minutes into our trip, Cassidy told me we needed to stop because she was having some pretty serious cramping, and she wanted to go to the restroom to check. We stopped at the McDonald's off the Clinton, South Carolina exit in hopes that everything was still on track and that nothing traumatic was about to happen. Obviously, I couldn't go into the women's room with my wife, but I was fighting the urge to do it. The next few minutes waiting outside seemed like an eternity, and the expression on her face when she came out made it worse.

Our short-lived exuberance over Cassidy's pregnancy was over. Cassidy had a miscarriage which, on its own, is deeply emotionally painful, but to experience something so awful in a McDonald's restroom off the interstate added insult to injury. We just sat in the car and held one another, both in tears, before we decided to finish the trip home to try and move on and mourn the loss together. We held hands for the remainder of the trip, and both of us were stunned into near silence.

The next few weeks would be the toughest part of the experience. The differing ways in which we coped with the loss divided us at a time when we needed one another most. I decided to throw myself back into my work. Cassidy decided to seclude herself at home to work through all of it on her own. Neither of us fully appreciated the way in which the other dealt with a tough loss. I thought that secluding ourselves would only make matters worse while Cassidy felt like I was emotionally shut off instead of just facing everything head on. After months of this stalemate, we finally reconnected with one another and agreed that we would not force the issue of getting pregnant again. Instead, we decided to focus on our marriage and on getting past the stress of that spring and early summer.

CHAPTER 5

PREGNANT AGAIN

W e lost our first baby in spring of 2010, and we found out we were
pregnant again in November of that same year. For us, the first
full year of our marriage had been filled with enough ups and downs to
last a lifetime; we were both exhausted. Learning that we were pregnant
again elicited differing emotions in both of us after the sadness we had
experienced in the spring.

We learned that we were pregnant at an election-night party for
current South Carolina Governor Nikki Haley. Due to my involvement
in the 2010 governor's race through the policy foundation I chair, we
had been invited to election night events in downtown Columbia. Because I had taken a position with a bank back home in the Upstate, this
would be one of our last hurrahs while living in Columbia.

Immediately after our wedding in October 2009, we moved to Columbia for a temporary work assignment and so that we could be closer
to the capital during the 2010 governor's race. Most of the events of our
early marriage had taken place in Columbia, but we both felt that it was
now time to move our home closer to our families in the Upstate. Little
did we know, our family would grow once we moved.

At the election-night party on November 6, 2010, Cassidy and I
joined my friend Chad Connelly, the incoming chairman of the South

Carolina Republican Party, and his wife for the festivities. Cassidy had been feeling a little nauseous most of that morning, but the symptoms seemed to have faded by early afternoon. As we were walking past a fellow on the street near the venue in Columbia who was smoking a cigarette, she began gagging. The smell of that cigarette nearly made her vomit which we all knew was not normal.

I quipped, "You are so pregnant," which I had no idea was actually true. I thought I was just being funny, a little light humor about a subject over which we had been so somber for so long. As the night went along, more scents and more reactions made me second guess what I thought was a joke.

The weekend after the election, we decided to do a pregnancy test while we were home visiting with our families in Spartanburg. It took mere minutes for the test to boldly render a positive verdict. My first reaction was excitement, followed almost immediately by fear. I was fearful of a miscarriage repeat, which both of us couldn't emotionally handle. I was fearful that Cassidy would drift even further from me now that she was pregnant again.

Once we got through Christmas and into the New Year, I felt that we were largely out of the woods from the standpoint of having a miscarriage repeat. Once we started visiting the OBGYN in January of 2011, I felt confident that Cassidy and I were going to become parents. The fear of losing our child was fading, but my fear of losing our marriage was growing.

Despite my disappointment with being less connected with Cassidy during her pregnancy than I had planned, I tried to remain positive and keep my relationship with my wife alive. I tried to encourage her to keep the romance between us alive and to keep the newlywed spark between us burning bright.

When it came time for the gender-reveal ultrasound, all of us were giddy. I was sure I would be happy with a boy or a girl, but I was so hopeful that my first child would be a son. I had dreamed of what it would be like to have a little boy to teach how to throw a baseball, swim, run through the woods, and more. I wanted a little buddy, and I saw him for the first time at an OBGYN clinic in Spartanburg Regional there on the ultrasound screen. I was elated, completely on cloud nine that, by summer, my son would be home.

After we learned that we were having a son and moved into a new place in Greer, South Carolina, equidistant from both of our families, my wife and I began to reconnect. It felt like we were recapturing some of the love and passion that had characterized our relationship during our dating, engagement, and early marriage. We began to act more like a team again, and I felt like we were beginning to form our own family. I was a blessed man with a woman I loved, a new job back home in the Upstate, and a little boy on the way.

Cassidy and I were excited about becoming parents, and we started decorating our son's future room with a new crib, stuffed animals, baby toys, and night lights. Some evenings, I would just go sit on the floor in our son's room and imagine what it would be like when he was born and came home to live with us. Having his room decorated made the pregnancy more real in my mind; we were *actually* going to be parents, and the day was quickly drawing near!

Even the process of naming our son was joyous. One of our favorite movies while we were dating was a classic medieval story of chivalry and romance that was recast in a modern movie starring James Franco. I have often described the movie as *Braveheart* meets *Romeo and Juliet* as it has elements of gallant chivalry and war (which makes the movie appealing to guys) and the star-crossed romance of Romeo and Juliet. My son's namesake is the main character, and he combines a charming combination of courage and class that we wanted our son to embody. I also wanted to pass on the family name to some degree, so we decided to name our firstborn son after a movie character and me.

The last weeks of Cassidy's pregnancy seemed perfect; I thought we had found our stride. We were both excited about our new baby boy, and we were beginning to reestablish our relationship and the passion that we had shared. It seemed like we were well on our way to becoming the perfect family. I was elated beyond description.

On the morning of June 12, 2011, which was a Sunday, my wife and I decided to sleep in and rest. We were close to full term, and we knew that we wouldn't have too many more weekends to spend alone sleeping in and reconnecting with one another. We had an intimate morning together before we finally decided to get up and make some breakfast. It was as I was cracking eggs to scramble that her contractions commenced.

By the time we were sitting down to breakfast, it was pretty clear that Cassidy was going into labor and that we needed to get to the hospital ASAP. I quickly gathered our "go bag", and we rushed to the car to get to the Brushy Creek campus of the Greenville Hospital System, which was about five miles from the apartment home we were living in off of Suber Road in Greer.

We arrived at the hospital around 11am that Sunday morning and began what we thought would be a very long day of labor and delivery. Fortunately for all involved, my son was ready to join us in the world, and he was born just a few short hours later at around 1:40pm that afternoon. He was the most beautiful little thing I'd ever seen, and I was instantly proud of and adored him.

The craziest part of the delivery day for me was cutting the umbilical cord and holding the little man for the first time. I was filled with awe at this little person I was holding and for whom I was now responsible. His little hands, sweet little face, and tiny little feet were unfathomable. I was immediately reminded of the passage from Jeremiah wherein the Lord said, "Before I formed you in the womb, I knew you."

Cassidy and I both spent about an hour alone with our son before our families were brought in a few at a time to see the newest addition to our family. Everybody, it seemed, immediately fell in love with him and that most certainly included his daddy. Little did I know that the heaven on earth we experienced on June 12, 2011 would become hell on earth by July 8th.

CHAPTER 6

THE END OF OUR CAMELOT

A lmost immediately after we returned home with my son, the fears
I felt about our marriage began to come to pass. Cassidy turned
back to her mom to help her make decisions for our son, from choice of
doctor to diet. I tried to be patient and understand that we had been
through a major life transformation that would take time to become normal. Nevertheless, after all we'd been through together, it did hurt me
that my wife didn't seem to want to include me in joint parenthood anymore.

The next three weeks were a bittersweet blur. My relationship with
Cassidy seemed to be fraying, but my attachment to my newborn son
was growing by the day. I would host my then-morning radio program
at 6:30am and then head to the office for the rest of the workday. I would
then rush home immediately after work to see my wife and son. In those
early weeks, we had a good bit of trouble sleeping as most parents do
and had to come up with a schedule that would work for all of us. Cassidy would wake up at regular intervals to breastfeed our son, which
required that we wake him up at each appointed time. Honestly, there
were times when it may have been easier on all of us if we had just waited
until the next time he was awake! Most evenings, my son would not
sleep in his crib, so he ended up in the bed with Cassidy and me and

would sleep right in the very center of my chest. He was like a little oven, and we all slept warm and cozy when my baby son was in the mix. The fact that he slept on my chest made it all the more difficult when he either woke up on his own or when his mom woke him up to feed him. I was awake with mom and son and still needed to go to the radio program and office the next morning!

My son had been home one week by the time Father's Day 2011 rolled around on June 19th. I was beaming that I was the new father of a beautiful baby boy and that I could actually claim to be a father on Father's Day for the very first time! Given that my son was just one week old on Father's Day, Cassidy understandably stayed home with him while I went to the church we were attending at the time—Taylors First Baptist outside Greenville—for the Father's Day service. I felt the overwhelming urge to pray for the upcoming challenges I would face as a new dad and for the little life for which I was now responsible. I had no idea how great those challenges would soon be and how much strength I would need to face the coming storm.

When I got home from church, Cassidy had prepared a nice little Father's Day lunch for us and had given me two sweet little cards, one from her and one from our son. In both, she wrote beautiful messages about how supportive I had been during her pregnancy and how proud she was to watch me interact with our little son. She even complimented me for praying with him before bedtime and prior to meals even though he was much too young to understand it. Her loving words were so inspirational to me, and they made me feel that the seeming tension of the past couple of weeks would eventually dissipate and that we would, together, be parents to our baby boy. There were few men in the country any happier on June 19, 2011 than I. I was so blessed beyond words to have a beautiful wife, wonderful son, and a bright future ahead of us.

The next two weeks were a flurry of activity. I had taken a few days off around the time of my son's birth to ensure that I was there to support Cassidy and that I was there to greet little man when he arrived. On the Monday after Father's Day, it was back to my regular schedule with the radio and at the office. My weeks tend to be pretty crazy, with workdays starting well before 7am and running until around 7pm in the evening. This is largely because I'm a daily, conservative talk radio host in addition to being a commercial banker; it's basically double duty. Even though weeks normally rush by with my kind of schedule, I still tried to take it a little slower and be more attentive to home in those early weeks after my son was born. I would often come home during lunch or swing by between appointments to be sure that all was well on the home front.

Cassidy seemed to be relishing her role as a mother and truly enjoying staying at home with our son. She had been a hairstylist with a local salon well into her pregnancy, and we had discussed whether or not she would return after our son was born. At the time, being a single-income household would have been pretty hard. My income was good but not great, given that I had only been with the bank I worked for at the time for about four months. We both realized that major changes were going to have to be made, but we were not sure what to do about our need for two incomes, while also providing childcare for our son. Our decision at the time was to have Cassidy stay home with our son until we could figure out our next steps, an option she had by virtue of being a contractor, 1099 employee of the salon where she rented space.

The second week at home went almost as smoothly as the first. Cassidy seemed to be feeling great, and we were both so happy that our son was doing so well. At his first doctor's appointment at the children's clinic, his vital signs, weight, motor skills, etc. were in the top percentiles, and he was doing well with sleeping at night and taking his meals. Cassidy and I were seemingly on the same page and were adjusting to the fact that it was no longer just the two of us. Our young family was beginning to take shape, and despite all of the challenges and turmoil of the first 18 months of our marriage, it seemed that we were happy. All of this would change in week three of our son being in our lives.

As the calendar turned to July, there was no reason to suspect that our happy family was about to be shattered forever. The first week of July has, at least for me, always been one of the best times of the year. The Fourth of July has always been second only to Christmas on my list of favorite holidays. The patriotic Americana that has come to characterize Independence Day has always gripped me, and I've always loved the festivities, the fireworks and, yes, the big BBQs that accompany the summer celebration. I figured the Fourth in 2011 would be particularly special, considering I now had a new baby boy and a wife with whom I was a new parent. This would change when what Cassidy and I believed were belated pregnancy complications arose the weekend before the Fourth, which was on a Monday in 2011.

Cassidy and I were at home with our son in Greer on Saturday evening, July 2nd, when I decided that I wanted to take an after-dark run down Wade Hampton Boulevard, given that it was still so very warm out with the summer air. I laced up my running shoes to hit the road and planned to go for a three-mile run down the busy thoroughfare that ran through the Greer community. As the tension between Cassidy and me was rising a bit due to the normal pressures of being new parents plus the constant presence of her mom, I needed to run to refresh myself to stay committed to helping my wife as we learned what it meant to be new parents.

Right before I left to run that evening, we had a bit of an argument over our respective parenting styles. To add to that argument, Cassidy kept claiming that she wasn't feeling well. She was experiencing some sharp pains in her lower abdomen and her pelvic areas. Given that she had given birth just three weeks prior, we both thought this may be the beginning of some post-delivery complications. After ensuring that she was comfortably situated on our couch, I went out for a much-needed run. I have always loved running as it provides time to connect with God while listening to worship music and recharging my mental batteries. On this particularly evening, it was more needed than was normal.

After three hard miles, I came back to our third-floor apartment home to take a shower. I was ready for the next challenge after pounding the pavement for the past 20 minutes. Little did I know just how much I would need that newfound mental calmness. From the minute I walked in the door, the chaos ensued. Apparently, during the time it took me to go for a run, the pain in Cassidy's abdomen had significantly worsened. It seemed to me that the time to head back to the hospital had more than come. I told Cassidy I was going to take a quick shower, pack a bag for us, and begin getting our son ready so we could go to the hospital and figure out what was happening with her.

Within 30 minutes of my relaxing run, Cassidy, our son, and I were loaded up in the car to head to the Greenville Hospital's Brushy Creek campus and to the same ward where our son was delivered less than a month before. Cassidy was immediately readmitted to the maternity ward. The doctors agreed with us that it seemed like these symptoms were complications from the delivery of our son. The doctors decided to put Cassidy on intravenous antibiotics, something that made her even sicker than when we started. She always had sensitivity to antibiotics, and having them injected through an IV made her incredibly sick. Within an hour of arriving at the hospital, she was vomiting, had cold chills, had diarrhea, and could not get comfortable enough even to sleep.

All the while, I was in the hospital room with Cassidy, taking care of our son and trying to get him to go to sleep as it was already well past 10 p.m. It became pretty obvious when Cassidy went on the IV antibiotics that we would need to find a method other than breast feeding to feed our son during the hospital stay. I told the nurses that I was more than happy to feed him formula with a bottle, something they agreed to help me do as a stopgap measure. This raised a sore point between Cassidy and me that had been festering since our son was born. I had always believed that we should help our son learn how to take a bottle in case of events like the one we were now experiencing when she would be unable to breastfeed him. I also thought that it may help take pressure off of Cassidy from feeling that she had to feed him herself every time he was hungry. With him being only trained to breastfeed, Cassidy had to be available at all hours of the day and night to feed him.

Almost immediately after I told the nurses I would happily feed our son with a bottle, Cassidy began to object. She also immediately called her mother, Kassandra, to come and help us at the hospital. Cassidy had her mom bring some organic goat's milk formula to feed our son instead of the formula the maternity ward nurses and doctors had recommended for us to use. They also told the nurse how they were worried about our son's future ability to breastfeed if he learned to take a bottle. To this day, I believe that these objections had less to do with sincere concerns over the healthiness of the formula and more to do with Cassidy's desire to have our son be dependent upon her to feed him as having me feed him with a bottle would undermine her control of the parental dynamics. That was certainly how the hospital staff and I viewed the objections of Cassidy and her mother that evening and morning in the hospital.

Finally, the nursing staff helped us to bridge the gap and end the impasse. They recommended that I feed our son with a syringe and feeding tube that we would attach to my finger. The thinking was that, if he felt the tip of my finger in his mouth, he would still react as if he was breastfeeding, which would make it easier for him to return to breastfeeding after our hospital stay was over. So, the hospital staff worked with me to make this new feeding system work.

That was an interesting experience, feeding my infant son with my finger and a feeding tube. I was just happy to help in any way possible and to take care of our son while my wife was trying to recover from whatever had gone wrong with her after delivery. I would mix the formula, put it into a cup, and then load it into a syringe. My son would then latch onto my finger with the feeding tube attached, and drink his milk almost exactly like he would if he were still being breastfed. He hated the goat's milk formula Kassandra had picked up, however, and we ended up using the formula that the hospital staff recommended, much to my mother-in-law's and my wife's dismay. I wasn't trying to pick a fight; I was just trying to make sure our son was taken care of while Cassidy was recovering.

The first day in the hospital ended with more questions than answers. The doctors were baffled as to what was going wrong. They had administered the antibiotics out of the belief that the pain she was experiencing was an infection from the delivery and that this would be enough to clear up the issue. The sickness that the antibiotic regimen brought led them to the belief that maybe she had developed meningitis, something that we both believed was unlikely, given that the sickness seemed pretty clearly related to the antibiotic administration. Nevertheless, the doctors decided that they wanted to do a spinal tap to rule out any chance of meningitis or other viral infection.

In came the doctors from the operating room with a spinal tap kit, which contained what had to be the single largest needle I had ever seen in my life. They had Cassidy sit on the side of the bed while I held our son and looked on. They inserted the needle into her spine. She winced in obvious pain, and a tear rolled down her check. I felt so very sorry for her and wished there was something I could do to take the pain away from her and take the whole family home again. After the spinal tap was completed, the doctors took the sample off to the lab to test for meningitis and other viral infections which they hoped might be the key to understanding the pain Cassidy was experiencing.

The tests came back negative, which led to a further sense of bewilderment both for the medical team and for the two of us. We could not figure out what was causing such serious pain and why we couldn't find its source. By Monday, July 4th, we had been in the hospital for several days, and emotions were running high. My mother-in-law's presence and insistence on my following her feeding methods and other instructions had put me on edge. As a result, Cassidy and I were angry with one another. Finally, Kassandra decided she would go home, which was a major source of relief—at least, for me. I decided to try to make Independence Day as special as I knew how for Cassidy so that it would ease some of the frustration with her hospitalization during the holiday. I brought BBQ from a local barbecue restaurant that was a major sponsor of my radio program and decorated her room with American flags, bunting, and brought from home our copy of *The Patriot.*

My son had stayed with me at the hospital on Saturday night, at our house with me and my mother-in-law (who slept in the guest bed) on Sunday night, and with my mother-in-law on Monday night. My mother wanted to keep him as well, but Cassidy was angry at the prospect, so we only let him stay with Cassidy's mom. He was back with me by Monday evening. The poor little fella was just as stressed as we all were, and it showed in that he was not sleeping as well as he had been and was much more easily upset than he had been during those first three weeks at home. We all wanted Cassidy to feel better, and I certainly wanted it for my son as well as for my wife.

By Tuesday morning, I think the doctors had all but given up trying to figure out what had seemingly gone wrong during delivery. Every test came back negative for every infection, virus, or bacteria for the medical team had tested. Cassidy's condition didn't seem to be worsening, but the pain still had not been alleviated, and none of us knew why. Even still, by Tuesday afternoon, the hospital told us that they were going to send us home on Wednesday and that we should come back if the situation seemed to worsen or if the pain did not subside within a few days.

Sure enough, on Wednesday afternoon, Cassidy was released from the Greer Memorial Hospital and was sent back home with nothing more than a few medications meant to ease the pain that she was feeling. Neither she nor I believed that the hospital stay had been at all effective, and the same pain that she had felt Saturday evening was still throbbing in her pelvic areas. We knew that relief would have to come from some-where, and we began looking up the names of various doctors and clinics around Greenville that we thought may be able to provide some answers as the hospital system seemed to have none. I called a doctor friend of mine from our church whom I trusted implicitly. He had been out of full-time practice for some time, but he still had many connections in the area with good, capable doctors that he trusted.

Despite my efforts to help, my mother-in-law found a non-medi-cally-licensed naturopath off of Augusta Road in Greenville. This "clinic" specialized in herbal and non-medical remedies to, it claimed, a range of medical problems. I was skeptical to say the least, but Kassandra had already made the appointment even though my health insurance plan, on which I paid for coverage for Cassidy and our son, did not cover the costs. Despite my protest, both Kassandra and Cassidy wanted to visit this clinic, so we all piled into cars and drove 20 minutes across town to see a person that could probably best be described as a witch doctor. They, in effect, read Cassidy's palm with an electrometer, claim-ing that imbalances in the body could be diagnosed through this method.

After 20 minutes at this non-medically-licensed clinic, we left with a bag of herbal teas, supplements, and other homespun remedies that were supposed to cure the inflammation in Cassidy's pelvic area. I had no confidence that these supplements would work, but I was merely try-ing to maintain a delicately-balanced peace at this point and to make sure that my son was okay while we tried to figure out what was wrong with his mother. Even after taking these supplements, the pain seemed not to fade, and the relief that Cassidy sought still could not be found.

The next day—Thursday, July 7th—would be my first day back to the office after Cassidy's symptoms had started, and it would prove to be the last full day of our relationship. While I had to return to the office, Cassidy's mother decided to come over to our apartment and help her with our son during the day while I was at work. At this point, my wife was still adamant that she did not want my mother anywhere around— for reasons I never could understand—but I was not about to start a fight over it given her fragile state and the need for our infant son to have constant supervision and care. As I left home that morning, her mother was on her way to spend the day with her and our son. She brought along Cassidy's 11-year-old sister whom she homeschooled.

Even though her mother was there, I tried to call and check on Cassidy and our son as often as I could. I was still very worried about my wife, and I missed being there to help with our baby boy while she was unable to care for him on her own. Nevertheless, I had already taken so much time off for my son's birth that I needed to catch up at the office and be sure that I was providing for my family financially. It was a tough balance to strike between being present at home while things were tough and also making sure I was doing my job so that I could take care of the hospital bills and keep us sheltered and fed. I was starting the really feel the stress, too, which only added to the tension that was building on the home front.

When I got home that evening, Cassidy started telling me about how wonderful of a job her mother was doing taking care of her and how sweet she was toward our son. While I was obviously happy that my wife and son were getting good care while I was gone, the message was pretty clear that her mother was doing a good job and that I was not. As I had done for much of the prior week, I tried to be supportive of Cassidy and our son, but I did express my frustration that, while I was trying to balance being at home and doing my job, it didn't seem that it was appreciated. I felt like all of the things I had done and was doing to help her through this tough time and to take care of our son during it all was completely overlooked in favor of her mother's involvement.

The next morning—Friday, July 8th—Cassidy told me that her mom was going to come over again to watch our son and take care of her while I was at the office. Again, I didn't object despite some misgivings about the state of our relationship and the fact that my family was largely frozen out while all of this was ensuing. I left for the office, and my mother-in-law came over to spend the day with Cassidy and our son, along with her 11-year-old daughter. We were now nearly one week into this ordeal that we still could not figure out, and the tension between Cassidy and me—as well as between our families—was reaching fever pitch. I felt like some sort of a conflict was coming. I just didn't know how it would all play out.

At lunchtime on that fateful Friday, I decided to go home and check on mom and son and to make sure that all was well with my family. Instead of scheduling a customary client lunch, I asked my assistant manager to watch the office for me while I drove across town to check on Cassidy and our son. When I arrived, it was as if I had intruded into my own home. Instead of being happy to see me, Cassidy seemed genuinely irritated that I had even made the trip. She was lying on the couch, holding our son, while her sister and mother were working in the kitchen. It was as if they were trying to stay out of the way while Cassidy told me something important.

Within a few minutes, my wife was telling me how she wished I would take care of her like her mother did and that I was doing a terrible job of looking after her and our son. Her words were like gut punches to me, and I was deeply hurt. I was trying my best to balance work and home and to ensure that I was meeting my family's needs. I will never claim that I was the perfect husband who never made mistakes, but I was trying my best to be there for Cassidy and our son, and I felt like the constant presence of her mother and sisters was making that all the more difficult and awkward. After a few minutes of Cassidy telling me how much better her mother was at taking care of her than I was, I apologized and left to return to the office.

The entire drive back to the bank felt like a blur. I had tried so hard to be there for my wife every step of the pregnancy, post pregnancy, parenting, and the medical complications afterward. I desperately wanted to be both a good husband and a good father, and I thought I was doing a decent job on both fronts. I loved my wife and son, and I was doing everything that I thought I should to provide for them and be there for them as we adjusted to our new lives together. I was overwhelmed and stressed out like Cassidy was, and now she was telling me how much I was failing her and our son. It was heart-wrenching as well as angering. I didn't know if Cassidy had come to these conclusions all on her own or if her mother had guided her along the course to these convictions. All I knew was that Cassidy and I were further apart than at any point in our marriage, and it seemed to have happened almost overnight.

Back at the office, I tried to reapply myself to my work and let the tough time I'd had with Cassidy at lunch fade from my mind. We had both been through a lot, and I assumed the stress of the past few weeks was normal. I hoped it would get easier and that we would find our footing when it came to co-parenting. I hoped that our families would finally find the proper balance and boundaries.

A few hours after I got back to the office, Cassidy gave me a call. When I saw the call coming in, it gave me encouragement; I assumed that she was calling to apologize for how our lunch went and to clear the air from the tension we had both felt over the past few days. But when I answered her call, my wife was short and curt. She told me that I needed to stop by the store on the drive home to pick up mayonnaise and a few other items that her mother needed for the dinner she was preparing at our place. This meant, of course, that my mother-in-law was going to be staying for dinner, something that I utterly dreaded. The last thing that my family needed after half a week in the hospital, the full week on edge with Cassidy still hurting, the two of us fighting, and her mother a constant presence was for Kassandra to stay for dinner. I didn't want to start another fight with my wife, but I also wanted to try to change the plans. I told her that I would happily pick up dinner for us on the way home so that we both could relax, her mother could go home and rest (and leave us alone), and we could recalibrate after the crazy week that we had just been through. This suggestion didn't go over well, and Cassidy was adamant that dinner with her mom was going to happen.

On the drive home that evening, I honestly forgot to swing by the store before I got back to our apartment. I was just ready to be home and, hopefully, to reconcile with Cassidy and see my son. I let it slip my mind to stop for mayonnaise for my mother-in-law's chicken salad—not that I was all that disappointed. When I walked in the door, the scene was almost a repeat from what I had seen at lunch. Cassidy was still on the sofa recovering in the living room with our son lying on her arm. My mother-in-law and her youngest daughter were in the kitchen, making a meal. It seemed that my forgetting the mayo for the chicken salad was not too much of an issue as they were making some sort of stir fry that didn't seem to require it. Kassandra told me that she had made a plate for me as well, which was a kind gesture even if I was irritated by her still being there. I told her "thank you" and that she didn't need to feel like she had to make me dinner; I was sincerely trying to be appreciative. She took offense to what I said, and responded, "Well, of course I was going to make it for you, too!" I think she took my deferential statement literally and thought I was being critical of the fact that she had made a plate for me as well.

After thanking Kassandra again, I grabbed my plate and walked into the living room to see Cassidy and to eat near her so that we could be together for a few minutes. The moment I sat down beside the couch on which she was lying, she snapped and said, "You were really hateful to my mom just now." I was a bit taken aback; I thought I had been kind considering I just wanted a few minutes alone with my family. It seemed that Cassidy had heard the exchange between her mother and me and was of the opinion that my deferential statement about Kassandra not needing to prepare dinner for me was hateful and disrespectful. I told her that I did not understand and that I was not trying to be rude or mean to her mother. Nothing that I said seemed to matter as she grew more and more irritated, telling me how I was disrespectful to her mother and that I didn't even care about her and my son.

By this time, I really couldn't take any more of the negativity. We were all on edge, and I was trying to be understanding of that fact. Nevertheless, I was also tired of being constantly criticized when I was doing my best to be supportive. In the midst of this argument, Kassandra and her daughter left to go back home to Simpsonville. I told Cassidy that I was leaving to clear my head and that I was tired of fighting with her and arguing about her mother's constant presence. I told her that I felt she was constantly deriding me, ignoring what I was doing to help her and our son, in favor of her mother's constant presence. I understood her desire to have her mom around during these tough times, but belittling and alienating me was hurtful and, honestly, made me pretty angry. I took my keys and headed down to my car to clear my head for a moment.

I decided to go to the store to get some chicken salad because Cassidy had asked me to get mayo earlier in the day so that her mom could make it. I also bought some soap and other household items that I knew we needed. I rented a few movies that I thought she and I could watch when I returned back home. Despite our fight, I was hopeful that we could regain our footing and that we could have a good night of reconnecting after a week from hell. After paying for these items at the store near our home, I headed straight home, recharged and ready to make things right on the home front. When I got upstairs to the apartment, I found that my plans had been dashed.

Cassidy was packing her bags, and she told me that she was leaving. I was stunned. Leaving? For how long? To go where? Her response was that she was through with our marriage and that she was moving back to her parents' house, presumably with our son. She said that she was tired of our marriage and how I treated her, our son, her mother, family, etc. and that she was ready to move back home. It was the strangest, saddest thing I had ever experienced in my life. Just two weeks prior, on Father's Day, she had written the sweetest card to me about how I was the most amazing husband and father that any women could ever dream of being married to and that she was "blessed among women" to be my wife. Now, she was telling me that she had never been happy in our marriage and that she was going to move with our son to her parents' house.

I had no idea how to react. I certainly didn't intend for her to leave our apartment with our son, permanently leave our marriage, and live again with her parents. I told her that, if she left, I would do everything I could to retain custody of our then three-week-old son. I didn't intend to lose my son because she had suddenly decided she didn't want to be married any longer. It seemed like this really fired her up as she began packing our son's clothes and supplies in her suitcase with her clothes. She informed me that she had already called her entire family to come and help her move out of our apartment. This wasn't something that she had decided on the spur of the moment. She had planned this for some time as she was taking all of her clothes and our son's clothes, and she had her family moving crew in route to make it all happen.

Honestly, I came unglued in that moment. I had no idea what to do. When I took my wedding vows on October 24, 2009, I meant them. When we recited the words of Ruth from the Old Testament, "Where you go, I will go, where you lodge I will lodge, your people will be my people, your God, my God", I meant them. I had never even imagined leaving or divorcing my wife. When I asked Cassidy how she could do this to our family… to us… she responded by saying that I walked out. I went to the store. She said I walked out. I was there begging her not to leave, not to destroy our family, and not to do this to our son. Yet she claimed that I walked out. When her family arrived, it was like pouring gasoline on a fire.

Her middle sister and her boyfriend, her mother, father, and youngest sister all piled into our apartment and began going through our things. They were helping her pack up our son's room, her clothes, formula, etc. as if this was just a routine move. I was in a combination of shock and anger. I was stunned that this entire family was packing my son's clothes, toys, and bedding right along with my wife's clothing and personal items. Just weeks after the cards, letters, and text messages praising me for being a good father and talking about how wonderful I had been to her as her husband, she was now packing up to leave for good… and taking my son from me on top of it. I was not prepared to just stand by and say nothing.

When Cassidy's sister's boyfriend started picking up my son's diaper bag and the stuffed elephant animal that I had bought for him (the first gift I ever gave my son), I couldn't stand by and say nothing any longer. I confronted him and told him that he was not welcome in my home and to put my son's stuff down. It got pretty heated, and the exchange between the two of us led to more tension between Cassidy, her family, and me. I felt like I was being ganged up on by my wife and her family. After standing by her through all that we had been through in our short marriage—especially through the miscarriage of our first pregnancy, her pregnancy with our son, and becoming parents—I couldn't believe that Cassidy was walking away from our marriage and was planning to take my son away from his father from infancy.

After years of reflection on Cassidy's abandonment of our marriage and subsequent attempts to take my son away from me, I have come to believe that it was premeditated. Every step that Cassidy took from July 8, 2011 portrayed me as an abusive husband and father who is an unfit parent. The rapid succession in which Cassidy took steps to file for separation and divorce, for financial support—not only for my son but for her car payments, student loan payments, cell phone payments—and for absolute custody of our son eventually led my lawyers and me to con-clude that this was possibly planned well before even our son was born.

CHAPTER 7

THE BATTLE BEGINS

Most states in the United States have dysfunctional family court systems driven by outdated family law codes, and this is especially true in my home state of South Carolina. I love my home state, and I believe we do a lot of things right in South Carolina; family law isn't one of them. Once two parents separate, there is an exceedingly high probability that the child or children over which they fight in a custody case will be relegated to government-mandated, single-parent childhood. From the moment a court gets involved, the likeliest outcome is that one parent—normally, the father—will have so-called *standard visitation*, which is every other weekend and one night per week. Meanwhile, the other parent will have primary legal custody along with about 80% of the time with the child or children and will receive child support from the parent that has largely been cut off from the lives of their children. This "solution" is extreme and unfair, yet it is typically decided in a 15-minute hearing known as a *temporary hearing* before a family court judge with no jury and no second opinion.

I would learn all of this the hard way through years of experience that began just weeks after my wife left our marriage. On the evening of July 8, 2011, I was a devastated man. My wife left me shortly after I got home that evening and took our month-old son with her. I couldn't get her to return any of my phone calls or text messages, and I couldn't figure out what had happened. We were seemingly in love just weeks before and were celebrating the birth of our baby boy. But by the evening of July 8th, the joy and the happiness of embarking on life together as a family was gone. In its place, there was the agony of love lost and devastation over the loss of my wife and my son being taken from me. I was still unwilling to accept this as final, and I resolved to do everything in my power to try and restore my marriage to Cassidy and bring her and my son home.

I truly believed that Cassidy might have some sort of post-partum depression based on the rapidity of her decision to leave our marriage only weeks after our son was born. Given that she had just given birth to our son and had been re-hospitalized for complications, I didn't think post-partum depression was an unlikely prospect. In the months leading up to our son being born, Cassidy's emotions were clearly becoming more intense. Though I had never experienced walking with a woman through pregnancy before, I did understand that hormones and emotions are at full throttle during pregnancy.

I tried to be understanding of Cassidy's emotions leading up to my son's birth and in the weeks after, but there were certain things she did that I was not so sure could be explained away as merely hormonally driven or part of post-partum depression.

A few months before my son was born, my wife attacked our neighbors—literally. We lived in a third-floor apartment during our pregnancy and through the end of our marriage. We lived in some very nice apartments in Greer only miles from the hospital where our son was born. Because we were short-term residents as we were looking for something more permanent once we became parents, we didn't get to know most of our neighbors in the apartment complex. We did, however, get to know the family that lived in the apartment directly beneath us, a late-30s couple with four young children. They were very kind people, and they were always on their patio, partly because their children were always outside playing and partly because the husband and wife both liked to smoke… often.

One evening in March before our son was born, my very pregnant wife and I were sitting in our living room at home one evening, relaxing before bed. She was watching a movie, and I was reading George W. Bush's new book, *Decision Points*. I thought we were having a perfectly pleasant evening even though Cassidy looked a little intense while she was watching her movie. Shortly after we sat down, we heard the neighbors below, walking out onto their balcony for their evening cigarette. A few minutes later, Cassidy began complaining about being able to smell the smoke coming from their patio, and she told me that I needed to go down there and tell them to put it out. I understood that she had a heightened sense of smell during her pregnancy, something we had learned the week we found out she was pregnant with our son, but I couldn't smell any smoke.

Cassidy was angry that I didn't immediately get up and go tell our neighbors to put out their cigarettes. I told her that, even though I couldn't smell their smoke, we could go into the other room and watch TV or go to bed but that I couldn't walk downstairs and demand that our neighbors not smoke on their own balcony. For the time, that seemed to settle the matter as she went back to watching her movie while I went back to reading my book. A few minutes later, however, she walked into the kitchen, seemingly irate. I decided to keep reading, hoping that a few minutes alone might help her to clear her head and calm down. I was wrong.

A few minutes later, I saw Cassidy walking back into the living room from the kitchen with the mop bucket in her hand. Initially, I had no clue why she was bringing the mop bucket into our carpeted living room… until I saw her heading toward the balcony door. It all seemed to happen in slow motion. She opened the door with soapy water sloshing over the sides of the mop bucket and walked out onto the balcony. Seconds later, she dumped the entire bucket of soapy water on the couple below. I immediately heard the husband cursing and thought we might have a problem. When Cassidy walked back in and closed the door behind her, I asked, "What the hell did you do?" She simply said nothing. She just sat back down on the couch and resumed watching her movie.

I heard the pounding feet coming up the wooden stairs. My neighbor, while a nice person, was a bodybuilder-type guy. Despite his chain smoking, he did go to the gym for weight training virtually every day. While I am in pretty good shape, and I think I could hold my own if forced to, I did not want to get into some sort of fight with the fella down below. Nevertheless, as I heard his feet approaching, I assumed that was what was about to happen. Moments later, I heard the pounding on the door. I told Cassidy to go into the living room and stay out of sight while I figured out how to clean up the mess she had made. Slowly, I opened the door to see this angry guy covered in mop water, standing outside my door.

He was irate. That much was obvious, and I certainly didn't blame him. I asked him to take a step back so that I could come outside and talk with him, and he obliged. He began demanding to know why we had poured water all over him and his wife as well as their phones and other electronic equipment. It was a fair question, I believed, and I tried to explain that I was so very sorry and that my wife had made a very rash and irrational decision. He began to calm down to the point that I believed we had were going to at least avoid a trip to the hospital that evening, and I asked him what I could do to make amends. He simply requested that I replace his wife's new smartphone, which was saturated to the point that it would not turn on. I, of course, agreed, and I told him that I would come down later to talk with his wife and that they could just forward the bill for the new phone directly to me.

When I walked back inside our apartment, Cassidy was just staring at me with an icy glare. I told her that I didn't know what had gotten into her but that her actions had just cost us several hundred dollars and could have led to a much worse confrontation. I was stunned that she would act in such a way, and I told her that she owed the neighbors an apology. Eventually, she walked downstairs (I went with her to ensure that nothing got out of hand) and apologized to the couple. The family was so very gracious, and the fella and I became friends afterward.

When Cassidy and I got back upstairs, she was still cold toward me and actually blamed me for the entire episode. She said that if I had handled it the first time she asked, she would never have had to have taken the measures that she did. I couldn't believe it; I had to diffuse a potentially explosive situation she had created through rash actions, yet she blamed me for the fact that it ever happened in the first place. It was truly surreal. It was also a harbinger of things to come in which Cassidy would take irrational actions—such as leaving our marriage and taking our son—while blaming me for abandoning her first. That was exactly what she did the day she left our apartment with our baby boy on July 8, 2011.

In the days and weeks that followed, I sought ministerial advice, marriage counseling, and tried unsuccessfully to meet with Cassidy to discuss what went wrong. All she would ever tell me was that I had abandoned our marriage and that she went home to her family to find support. Of course, that was easy to disprove given that I lived in our apartment in Greer for nearly a year after she walked out that July and tried repeatedly to reconcile with her. Nevertheless, her standard argument to anyone who would ask was that I left her and our son to fend for themselves and that her mother and father swooped in to save the day. It was an alternate reality but one that I believe she actually convinced herself of as time drew on, despite all the evidence to the contrary. There was something going on with Cassidy that was much deeper than post-partum depression, but I had no idea what was happening.

That evening episode in March of 2011 was in the back of my mind as we went forward with Cassidy's pregnancy. It certainly was something I thought about during those tense weeks after my son was born as my wife seemed to harbor more and more resentment for me. By the time she was packing her and my son's clothes and moving home with her parents, I was convinced that there was a side to the woman that I had married that I was not comfortable with or aware of when we were dating. I would become the object of her ire in the months and years ahead, which would far outweigh the joyous and good times that we shared together.

In those first weeks after Cassidy left our marriage, I oscillated back and forth between believing that our marriage was over and that the character Cassidy exhibited in episodes like the one involving our neighbors was more the norm than the exception and believing that she was really going through a major bout of post-partum depression and that our marriage would be reconciled. I didn't fully believe that we would get divorced, fight a years-long battle for custody of our newborn baby, and that I would end up in jail in the process. July of 2011 was a seminal moment in my son's and my life. Everything I had hoped for both of us and for Cassidy was over in an instant.

Any hope that I still held for reconciliation ended on July 20, 2011. I was at home at the same apartment Cassidy accused me of abandoning, having dinner alone when I heard a knock on the door. A man whom I had never met was waiting at the door with a package in his hands. He told me he was a courier for a local law firm and that he was delivering papers for me from my wife's attorney. The moment that I had hoped wouldn't come and had fought to prevent had come in the form of a courier carrying divorce papers. I had listened to the advice of my marriage counselors who strongly suggested that I not take legal action against Cassidy as to do so would exacerbate and already delicate situation. We thought that Cassidy would eventually come around, and I didn't want to be the one to start a legal war. Despite my forbearance, I was now forced to lawyer up as the list of demands and accusations included in Cassidy's first court filing was long and exhaustive and filled with false allegations.

The battle had begun, and little did I know that it would take the next five years of my son's and my life to find any semblance of resolution.

CHAPTER 8

BLEEDING US DRY

A s I stood in my kitchen, reading through the first set of pleadings filed by Cassidy's lawyer, I was completely stunned. In these documents, the woman with whom I had hoped to reconcile demanded near-total custody of our son and only supervised visitation with him for me. They also demanded that I pay her cellphone bill, her car payment, continue paying her health insurance, and additional monies for other expenses. Her "justification" for such outrageous and excessive demands was that I had abandoned her and our son and abused them both. In the dozen or so attached pages, Cassidy literally accused me of trying to prevent her from breastfeeding our son, calling him fat and belittling him (he was three-weeks old), not paying attention in church, and not having a "teachable spirit" when it came to listening to her parenting advice. In that first set of pleadings, Cassidy threw the proverbial phonebook at me and tried to portray me as a heartless, horrible husband and father who was good for nothing… except paying all of her personal bills.

As I read through this document, I became convinced that there was no turning back. There would be no way to reconcile with someone who was so willing to slander my character, take my son away from his father, and gratuitously lie in an official court document. I would need legal counsel because Cassidy had just thrown down the gauntlet, and I had no choice but to prepare for a temporary hearing if I hoped to have any sort of ongoing relationship with my son. I had already been without seeing him for more than a few minutes at a time in a coffee shop with her family gawking on since Cassidy left on July 8th. I certainly had no intention of letting her have complete control over my relationship with my son.

At the same time, I still held out some hope that I might still be able to diffuse the standoff by, once more, being conciliatory and trying to avoid lawyering up. There was still part of me that believed this would all pass and that Cassidy would come home. In the long run, I believed this was the best thing I could do for all of us. If there was a way to prevent the marriage from completely collapsing and from having to take my son out of a nuclear family from the very beginning of his little life, I wanted to choose it. So, even after reading through this horrible set of allegations, I decided to represent myself at the first temporary hearing and, at least for the short term, give Cassidy most of what she was asking for in her pleadings. This would be contingent on a promise from her that she would cooperate with me on increasing my visitation with our son.

On the day of the hearing, I was nervous, but I had been assured by attorney friends of mine that, if Cassidy didn't live up to her promises to increase my access to our son and was completely unwilling to pursue reconciliation, I could always go back to court. This was a terrible mistake. I was acting in good faith with a woman that seemingly had absolutely no intentions of pursuing marital reconciliation and no intention of including me in the life of our son. My last-ditch attempt to save our marriage would, in the end, set me back all the more in a South

Carolina family court system that already marginalized dads in the first place.

When I arrived at our first temporary hearing, a Greenville County Family Court judge was presiding, and he seemed a little shocked that I came without an attorney. After reading through the laundry list of payments I had agreed to pay my estranged wife and the provision for her to have primary custody on a temporary basis, he seemed shocked. This certainly gave me no degree of comfort, but it was a little too late for me to bring counsel to this hearing. The court adopted the measures outlined by Cassidy's attorney which, of course, were very much to her favor. I left feeling used but still hopeful that my act of deference would spur Cassidy toward reconciliation, which I hoped would bring our entire family back together.

In the weeks after the temporary hearing, Cassidy became more belligerent toward me and less willing to work with me regarding visitation. Instead of softening after I showed good faith in the first hearing, Cassidy seemed to harden her heart all the more to the prospect of attending marriage counseling or reconciliation. Instead of increasing my visitation with our son, she further tried to limit my relationship with our son and my visitation. When I did get to see him, it was in a coffee shop called Java Jolt on the outskirts of Greenville. After weeks and weeks of occasional visits in a crowded coffee shop, which did not provide any real opportunity for me to bond with our son, I decided something had to change. None of my overtures to Cassidy were working, and my relationship with our son was suffering. I became convinced that my efforts to save our marriage had been in vain and that my focus must shift toward salvaging my relationship with my infant son. He needed his father as much as I wanted to be with him.

I finally relented and hired a Greenville attorney with a reputation for being as aggressive in the courtroom as any lawyer in the state in family-court cases. His resume was long, and his experience in the field was even longer. Buoyed by confidence in this man's credentials, I quickly paid the hefty retainer fee to have him read through Cassidy's laundry list of allegations and prepared a response to the pending temporary-hearing court date. I did not want it to come to this where Cassidy and I were litigating custody of our son and hammering out terms for a divorce, but it had been thrust upon me. My months of overtures had fallen on deaf ears, and the fact that she had compiled such a thick set of pleadings just two weeks after walking out our front door led my new attorney to believe that it was a premeditated act she had planned for many months.

I forced my emotions aside along with my pining to put back together the pieces of our broken marriage. As much as I still missed Cassidy, I was not about to allow her to deprive me of my son, now would I allow her to deprive my son of a relationship with his father. The legal system was now where we would find whatever resolution was to come after Cassidy abandoned our marriage, and I was pretty confident that it wouldn't be reconciliation any longer. My counsel recommended that we use two primary pieces of evidence in the temporary hearing which he believed would undermine her credibility and expose her allegations as false. We selected the affidavit from the neighbors she had assaulted on our balcony in March and the four-page note included in the Father's Day card that Cassidy had given to me on June 19th.

The logic behind submitting these two pieces of evidence was that they both spoke of her state of mind and credibility. The fact that she had recently assaulted our neighbors was, in our minds, a major red flag with regard to her rationality while the flowery Father's Day card written just a month before her lawsuit was filed completely contradicted the characterization she painted of me in her pleadings. With the temporary custody and separation hearing scheduled, I felt confident that I would easily dispatch with Cassidy's trumped-up case and that this nightmare would all be over soon. I was so very wrong.

I was still pretty naïve as to how prejudiced the family court system in our state is against fathers. It was my belief that the court would dismiss Cassidy's ludicrous claims as she had absolutely no evidence to back up her allegations, save sympathetic affidavits written by her immediate family members, while I had evidence written by her own hand that contradicted her own assertions.

On the morning of the hearing, my attorney and I arrived at the Greenville County Family Court just before the announcer called our case before the judge to begin the hearing. I still felt confident that we would prevail, especially after my attorney stood and delivered a rebuttal to Cassidy's outrageous claims and called for the judge to grant more custody to me. He explained that my weeks of trying to make it work after the first hearing were in vain and that it was now time for the court to grant me at least standard visitation.

Cassidy's attorney was prepared for our request for at least standard visitation and unloaded the latest round of allegations his client had compiled. Instead of just rebutting the allegations she had made during the first hearing in which I had represented myself, we were being hit with a whole new bag of lies. Her attorney stood and began explaining why Cassidy was going to move to deny the motion and told the court that I had engaged in disturbing behavior with our infant son. Cassidy, through her lawyer, claimed that I had held our son over a boiling, hot pot of water and had held him over a red-hot stovetop eye. These allegations were piled on top of all the prior allegations that she had made, claiming everything from that I didn't want to feed our son to that I had thrown paper towels in his face just to be mean.

These were lies for which she had not one shred of evidence aside from affidavits she and her mother had written against me. She had never before mentioned any of these supposed "disturbing behaviors" before in any emails, police reports, DSS filings, or even court documents. She fabricated them after I filed a counter claim to her near-sole custody and the financial package that I was paying for her personal comfort. She had lowered the boom on me just weeks after she abandoned our marriage, and she was now taking the allegations to the next level because I was pushing to have visitation with our son. She seemed pretty determined that I would not be part of his young life as her affidavits to the court made clear.

Of course, my attorney and I objected to the absurd claims that Cassidy clearly decided to make as an act of desperation now that I was finally fighting back against her efforts to alienate me from my son. We made the argument that they had no basis in fact and that they were just more of the same finger pointing in an attempt to win custody. The only thing Cassidy did to try and backup these allegations was to get her mother, who was certainly not an inactive or unbiased observer, to sign the statement with her. The judge looked utterly confused and downright frustrated. Instead of issuing a ruling that day, the judge said he needed time to read through the claims and would then issue a ruling as to temporary custody and child support. I left the hearing not knowing what to think but with confidence that Cassidy's malicious claims were completely unsubstantiated.

The next day, I was in Columbia for some political meetings that had been scheduled long before my hearing and was in a lunch meeting when I got a call from my attorney's office. The judge had handed down his ruling, and I was not going to like it. Instead of granting me the basic standard visitation that most non-custodial parents receive (which I still think is unfair to the child and to the parent), I was told that I could only have daytime visits every other Saturday with my parents as the supervisors. There could be no overnight visitation, and I could not take my son home with me. This was a tremendous blow to me.

I had done nothing but try to be an active and loving father, and my estranged wife was hell bound and determined to separate my son from me. Never once in our relationship or marriage had I abused or hurt my wife, and I never even imagined harming my own child. Yet my wife and her attorney were portraying me as a monster for no other reason than that she wanted more financial support and full custody. That was, in itself, infuriating. That the court would buy into these lies just because they were lodged by my son's mother was another thing entirely. Without any evidence outside her own assertions and without any basis in fact, Cassidy managed to use the legal system to get financial support with no strings attached and to cut off my relationship with my son.

Up until this point in the struggle to see my son, I thought Cassidy was my primary obstacle to being an active and engaged parent to my little boy. After this first hearing in which each side had lawyers, I quickly came to realize that, while Cassidy was certainly playing the part of the adversary, her greatest ally and my greatest obstacle was a family-court system that placed no premium on the role of a father. I also became convinced that my first attorney's complete lack of preparedness in the courtroom and failure to anticipate and respond to the allegations leveled by Cassidy and her attorney meant that I needed to make a change.

The first gentlemen I had hired had one heck of a reputation but was seemingly past his prime. While his services were not what they once were, his prices were as high as ever, and I was paying exorbitantly for counsel that led me into supervised visitation with my little boy. Though I had done nothing wrong with regard to my son, nor did I leave my wife, I was being treated like the bad guy. There was no sense of justice in our family-court system, and I felt like I was being persecuted and punished just for wanting to be an active parent to my only son.

Within a few days of that disastrous hearing in which Cassidy lodged her first allegations of child abuse against me, I relieved my first attorney of duty. A pastor friend of mine and his wife, who had gone through numerous family-court proceedings when they were trying to adopt their children, recommended an excellent family lawyer in Greenville who they believed I would appreciate. He told me that she would share my Christian values, unlike my prior attorney who had spent half of my last appointment with him (for which he was charging me $250 per hour) lecturing me for being pro-life and telling me how naïve I was for opposing late-term abortion. He also assured me that, in addition to being a person of principle, this attorney was incredibly skilled at winning family-court cases even on behalf of deserving fathers. I immediately called her office to schedule a consultation.

One meeting was all it took for me to ask Vanessa Hartman Kormylo to become my attorney. I had no idea how invaluable she would prove to be in the years to come or how great of friends we would become in the process. Vanessa is a person of acute intellect and unwavering integrity. These are not characteristics most of us would use to describe most attorneys, but Vanessa breaks the mold. I knew that, in order to prevail in my fight to be a parent, I would need someone who actually believed in the cause of their clients while also being professional enough to perpetuate an effective legal campaign to win a custody case.

Immediately after asking Vanessa to represent me, we started collecting statements from witnesses, counselors, and clergy that discredited Cassidy's ludicrous allegations of child abuse. We crafted a legal argument that highlighted my estranged wife's complicated history with the truth and her sudden allegation of abuse that she never claimed or reported until we were in a contested court case. Within weeks, we were headed back to court to end the insanity of having supervised visitation and to restore regular visitation to me as my son's father. When we went back to court, Cassidy's allegations fell apart. Vanessa had requested more than standard visitation as a means of reparation for the restricted relationship with my son that resulted from Cassidy's leaving and her fabrications in the first temporary hearing.

Vanessa and I also requested that a guardian ad litem be appointed by the court to fully investigate all claims made by Cassidy and report back to the court. We felt confident that, once Cassidy's claims were investigated and scrutinized, we would be in a better position to move toward shared parenting. Standard visitation between my son and me began, but we were hoping that we would be able to move the pendulum back in my direction and that, at very least, we would be able to get to joint custody and near-equal visitation with our son. After we went back to court and actually challenged Cassidy, the battle resumed. No one knew just how long and drawn out this case would become... or how public.

Even after the newly-appointed guardian ad litem met with us on multiple occasions, Cassidy maintained the allegations and piled on even more. During the weeks we met with this court-appointed guardian, Cassidy even started claiming that, when I changed our son's diaper, I wiped his bottom too hard because I was a clean freak. Her claim was that this was causing chaffing and was just more proof of abuse and yet another reason why she should have absolute custody and that I should never see our son more than on a supervised basis. At one point, probably because no one seemed sold on her constant stream of allegations, she brought our son to the guardian's office to take off his diaper, show her his bottom, and claim that he had a diaper rash that I had caused. The guardian, I am sure, was stunned. First of all, my son had been with her for visitation for a day or two prior to him being brought to the guardian's office. In addition, there was no issue beyond a slight redness often associated with infant children wearing diapers for extended periods of time.

This relentless stream of allegations, I believed, would actually work to my advantage in the end. There was never any basis in fact for these crazy claims, yet she seemed to come up with a new one almost every week. The way in which she rolled out a new allegation every time her case seemed to be in jeopardy undermined her credibility with virtually everyone involved in her case. I'm still convinced that her first attorney felt that this case was getting out of hand, especially when we were informed that he had been relieved of counsel to Cassidy. She had gone out and found herself another attorney. To this day, I don't know for certain what prompted it, but I believe it had much to do with the constant claims she made and the lack of credibility they conveyed.

After the guardian ad litem had completed her investigation, she concluded that there was no basis for the endangerment claims made by my former wife. Even still, the bias against fathers continued on unabated. While the guardian recommended increased visitation for me, she still recommended that my former wife have roughly 80% of the time with our son and that she have primary custody. To me, this was a devastating blow. After my wife left me, tried to keep me out of our son's life, and lied about me mercilessly to ensure that I never saw him again, the family-court system was still working against me. My attorney and I decided to come up with a deal that would increase my visitation beyond standard, and I would pay a higher level of child support.

The tradeoff that we crafted worked, and I agreed to pay child support as if I was only getting standard visitation of every other weekend and one night per week. In exchange, I would have our son for two days during the off-week and three days every other weekend. While still not the level of fatherly involvement I had envisioned when my son was first born and my wife and I were still together, it was a dramatic improvement over mere standard visitation, which amounts to being a visitor to one's child every couple of weeks. I had, in effect, paid tribute of sorts just so that I could see my own son.

Shortly after this visitation structure was put into place, Cassidy's and my divorce was finalized. Because of the custody actions, the normal one-year separation had long since passed, yet our divorce was not finalized until August of 2013. Over two years had passed since Cassidy had left our marriage and our son had lost his family structure at the ripe-old age of one month. So many allegations had been leveled against me. So many specialists, guardians, psychologists, experts, and lawyers had been involved in a case that had grown infinitely more expensive and emotionally draining than my family and I could have ever imagined. But, in August of 2013, it seemed that it may all actually be over. Cassidy and I were no longer legally married, and a reasonable—though, still unfair—agreement had been reached that ensured my son would have the involvement of both of his parents despite their divorce.

By the late summer of 2013, it seemed that healing could finally begin and that we would be able to take stock of the events and circumstances of the past two years and find a path forward. Despite Cassidy's unrelenting aggression since the summer of 2011 and the fact that our marriage was forever irreconcilable, I was cautiously optimistic that we might find a way to work together in a civil manner to provide structure and stability for our shared son. The past was the past, and now, we had to pick up the pieces and move forward.

Unfortunately, what I thought was the end of a nightmare was only the beginning of something far worse than anything that had happened thus far. The brutal custody battle and the allegations leveled against me throughout it by a woman I once so deeply loved was child's play compared to what was coming now that the marriage was officially over. If separation was a seismic struggle, post-divorce would be gladiatorial combat.

CHAPTER 9

MY SON'S NEW "DADDY"

My son began and ended his visits with me in the lobby of the Greenville County Law Enforcement Center in front of several uniformed sheriff's deputies. During the two-year divorce proceedings and concurrent custody battles, my wife's family tried everything they could think of to damage my chances at shared custody. They attempted everything from allegations, affidavits, and outright lies to setting up confrontations at exchange points and calling to file police reports. The result of one particular exchange was that my attorney and I requested that all future visitation exchanges take place at the law enforcement center (LEC) to try and prevent Cassidy and her family from engaging in antics that served only to further strain relations between us and to upset my son.

The event that precipitated my request to move all visitation drop-offs and pick-ups to the LEC was in the summer of 2013. Cassidy's father, who had grown increasingly dishonest and belligerent throughout the custody struggle, was coming to all visitation exchanges to serve as Cassidy's "witness." Because my family lived in Spartanburg, and I resided in Greenville, it was impossible for them to join me for each and every exchange. As such, I was normally outnumbered going into these exchanges, and it was always a source of increased anxiety for me. I'm sure this anxiety was transferred onto our then two-year-old son. The closer the final divorce hearing became, the more agitated my soon-to-be former father-in-law seemed to become.

Given the rising tension the closer we came to the divorce and final custody order, I began requesting that friends and/or family join me for every visitation exchange. Cassidy and her dad had started making claims to their counsel about how I would threaten them at exchanges and that I was trying to provoke them while we were exchanging my son. I wanted witnesses that would be able to testify to the fact that these claims, like all the others, were fabricated to try and give Cassidy the upper hand in court. We were so close to finalizing the divorce and settling custody that I didn't want some ludicrous allegation at the last minute to start the crazy cycle all over again.

It all sort of came to a head one evening after my family and I had taken my son to the Isle of Palms near Charleston for a weekend. During a weekend visit in late July of 2013, my parents and I decided to take my son to the beach for a few days. I had never been able to take him anywhere on any sort of trip because he had been taken from me shortly after he was born. I relished the opportunity to watch him play in the sand and run around in the water's edge; it was an amazing trip. Visitation ended on Sunday evening at 6pm, and we left Charleston late morning the same day. Due to some traffic on the interstate coming home, we got back into Greenville shortly before time to exchange him with Cassidy, so we went straight to a gas station near a local high school.

When we pulled into the parking lot, right on time, Cassidy was sitting in her car alone, awaiting our arrival. This was unusual because we were so used to her being there with her father who always seemed to want to engage in controversy for whatever reason. As my dad pulled our SUV up alongside Cassidy's car, we noticed that her father was sitting at a table inside the gas station, peering through the window as if he was making notes or recording the moment. For me, this was just ridiculous. What he thought he would gain by spying through the windows of a convenience store was beyond me, but it was annoying nevertheless. I went ahead and gave my son a goodbye hug and kiss after a wonder weekend at the beach and proceeded to give him to Cassidy so that she could put him in her car.

As Cassidy was getting my son settled in, I told my parents that I was going to go into the store to get some milk that I needed for the week. I ignored her father and went to the milk cooler, grabbed a half gallon, and got in line to pay for my purchase. Just as I was getting ready to step up to the counter, Cassidy's dad walked over to me and began telling me how much of an awful father that I am and how he was disgusted by the fact that I was on the radio every evening. This was a completely unnecessary and provocative verbal attack on me in a convenience store, all designed to elicit some reaction out of me that might help his daughter's case. I didn't take the bait but, instead, went ahead and paid for my purchase and went back out to the SUV where my parents were waiting.

A few minutes later, we watched as Cassidy's dad rejoined her in the car, and they drove off with my son as my parents and I began to pull out of the parking lot. While it was an infuriating event, nothing violent happened, no one was hurt or threatened to be hurt, and no altercation—other than Cassidy's father's verbal abuse—ensued. It was just another episode in a long train of such actions by my estranged wife and her family which I hoped would soon come to an end. While I never actually filed for divorce, I certainly did contest it after all of the allegations, and I knew that the divorce would be finalized within weeks.

The next morning, my lawyer Vanessa called me at the office. She asked if there had been an incident the night before at a convenience store near Riverside High School involving Cassidy, her father, and my family. Of course, I told her no and that her father had spouted off at me in front of the store clerk but that nothing of real note had happened. It turned out that Cassidy and her father had gone back to see the store clerk after my family and I had left the parking lot and told her that we were stalking them and trying to engage in a fight with them at the store earlier that evening. After getting the clerk's name and phone number, my former father-in-law called the Greenville County Sherriff's Office to file an incident report.

I was stunned. Despite all the wild things Cassidy and her family had done to try and push me out of my son's life, this was still a new low. Filing false police reports in hopes that the existence of such a report might hurt me in family court was a new low, even for this crowd. I told Vanessa what had actually happened, the police seemed completely uninterested in the entire episode, and nothing ever happened. I was afraid, however, that if we didn't change venues for exchange to a place with more accountability that this was all going to spiral out of control. Vanessa and I suggested that we conduct all future visitation exchanges in the lobby of the LEC so that false police reports wouldn't be a possibility anymore (or so I thought).

Both sides agreed, and beginning in the summer of 2013, my son exchanged visits with his parents in the lobby of the Greenville County Law Enforcement Center. The situation was so tense that officers recommended that, once we exchanged our son, the non-visiting parent would allow the other to get into his or her vehicle before walking out to get into his or her own vehicle to leave the premises. The entire situation was incredibly sad but was the result of Cassidy's continual false allegations and stop-at-nothing tactics to try forcing me out of our son's life. Even when our divorce was finalized, and the custody arrangement was formally in place concurrent with the divorce decree, my attorney and I decided that we would continue visitation exchanges at the LEC out of an abundance of caution.

On the first visit after our divorce was finalized in August of 2013, Cassidy brought a new boyfriend with her when she brought my son to visitation. His name was John, and apparently, the couple had met at a karate school where they both took lessons just down the street from where I lived. She made sure that John was holding my son in his lap when I arrived and that he was the one who brought my son into the LEC to hand him off to me. I couldn't help but believe that it was all designed to get under my skin and to send the message that, in her mind, my son had a new "daddy." But I didn't want to give the satisfaction of saying anything about it. I was determined not to be openly agitated or angry, but I certainly felt uncomfortable with this new fellow being so close to my son seemingly so quickly.

I had always believed that, when Cassidy or I started dating again, we should be careful about how quickly we introduced our new love interests to our toddler son. Given that our son had been torn from a nuclear family and forced into the center of a custody battle from his earliest days, I didn't believe that further confusing him with our personal lives was appropriate. As a result, I did not introduce my son to any women who I dated or even had dinner with unless it was in a casual context with other people around. I certainly never tried to encourage my son to believe that another woman was his mother or that he had a "new" family.

By December of 2013, just months after John made his first appearance at visitation, it was obvious that his relationship with Cassidy was much more than casual dating. On my birthday, December 18th, I had visitation with my son all day, as agreed upon in our visitation schedule. It was the single most-difficult day for me since the separation and divorce had begun back in 2011. Cassidy and John brought my son to the LEC that morning for my birthday visit. From the beginning, it had been obvious that Cassidy wanted my son to view John as his father. When they said goodbye to him, my son said to John, "Bye, Daddy," which my former wife did nothing to rectify or redirect.

Once I got my son strapped into his car seat, he immediately began telling me how John was his new daddy. At this point, my son was about two-and-a-half years old and already very verbal. He kept telling me that "John is my daddy" to which I would reply, "John is not your daddy. I'm your daddy. John is just a friend." As if on cue, he would immediately reply back, "No, John my daddy. Mommy say that John is my daddy." I was shocked and heartbroken. It was my birthday visit with my little son, and all he kept saying was that "John is daddy," something I knew he hadn't come up with on his own. It was clear that Cassidy had used my son to try and hurt me, and it worked. More importantly, she had further confused our son by teaching him that a man she had known for only months was his father.

During a weekend visit shortly thereafter, my son even told my mom that "John is my biological father." This was very clearly not the language of a two-and-a-half-year-old little boy but the spoon-fed lines taught to him by his mother and her new squeeze. During my birthday visit, I was so disturbed by the evident coaching of my son on what to say that I subtly videotaped him on my iPhone so that I could have video evidence to provide to my attorney. This was clearly a violation of our custody order and a clear escalation of Cassidy's attempts to freeze me out of my son's life even after our divorce was finalized.

The day after that sad birthday visit with my son, a friend of mine who worked for one of our U.S. Senators decided to look into Greenville County's marriage records to see if Cassidy was married and none of us knew about it. As it turned out, Cassidy and John Hatfield were married, and no one in my family or on my legal team knew about it. It seemed that my former wife married John within about 12 weeks of our divorce being finalized, had moved in with him and his family, and had already begun teaching my son that he was his new daddy.

What had seemed like the end of a nightmare back in August when our divorce was finalized had turned into the next chapter of an ongoing saga that would take a dark turn in the year ahead.

CHAPTER 10

A DIFFERENT STATE OF MIND

M y son and I rung in 2014 together at a wonderful New Year's party in Duncan. Cassidy's and my final divorce decree and custody order had allowed for our respective holiday visitation, with alternating schedules each year. In even-numbered years, I would have my son for the week leading up to Christmas and then through early afternoon on Christmas Day. In odd-numbered years, I would have my son for Christmas evening through New Year's Day. As such, I had my son as 2013 ended and we rung in a New Year filled with promise. With the divorce finally behind us and custody seemingly settled, I thought we could establish some semblance of normalcy in the year ahead.

I let my son stay awake that evening, and I was actually surprised that he stayed awake all the way to the New Year. One of my favorite photos from the 2013-2014 Christmas and New Year season was one of little man and me standing in front of the fireplace at our friends' New Year's party, holding a shining 2014 sign with my son's smiling face peeping out from behind the numbers. I had no idea what this year would hold, but with my son spending New Year's with my family and me, I felt pretty optimistic. With the divorce behind us and a custody agreement in place, it was time to find a new normal. I wanted my son to be sheltered from the fall-out of our failed family as much as possible.

I wanted him to know that he was loved by both Cassidy and me regardless of how she and I felt about one another.

Shortly after the New Year began, my dreams of a new normalcy were shattered. We learned in early spring that Cassidy was filing a motion in family court to allow her to relocate to Abilene, Texas. We were a mere six months into the final custody agreement that was filed when our divorce was finalized, and here was Cassidy already seeking to amend it. The petition she planned to file in court claimed that, after her marriage to John Hatfield, he enlisted in the U.S. Air Force and was going to be stationed at Dyess Air Base in Abilene after he finished his basic training. Cassidy intended to leave South Carolina to join him in Texas and requested that the family court give her complete custody. This meant that I would, at best, see my son 3-4 weeks per year, an outcome that I was absolutely unprepared to accept.

My attorney, Vanessa, and I were in disbelief. After all that my son had already been through, we felt that it was incredibly selfish for Cassidy to want to take him out of state and away from his entire family to live with a man to whom she had been married mere weeks after our divorce was finalized. While I completely understand the strains of military service on family units and applaud America's servicemen and women, I was unwilling to acquiesce to this request because it was brought about because of Cassidy's rash decision making. Knowing full well that we had a joint-custody agreement, she married a man who joined the military and needed to leave the state just three months after we were divorced. There was no way that my counsel and I were going to allow this petition to go to the court without protesting it and fighting it all the way.

Once Cassidy filed the motion to relocate, my team and I reached out to the guardian ad litem who had been assigned to the case. She was equally unsupportive of the prospect of Cassidy leaving South Carolina with our son and limiting his interaction with me to a few weeks per year. Cassidy's relocation proceeding seemed like it may have been running up against some pretty hefty headwinds for which I was thankful. I was hopeful that my son would be staying in South Carolina, regardless of the relocation decision that his mother may or may not make. My son and I had already missed too much time with one another during his short life, and I was determined that we would not go down that road again. Despite the headwinds, Cassidy would not be going quietly.

On a Friday evening, April 25, 2014, Cassidy took the entire custody case to a whole new level. April 25th was the weekend after Easter, and it was my weekend to have my son for visitation. I was excited because this would be my second weekend in a row to see my son. Because Easter is included on the Standard Visitation Holiday Schedule, it was my year to have him for Easter. As such, I was able to spend a long weekend with him the week before, complete with Easter egg hunts and church with our family. Now, less than a week later, I was supposed to see him again for my regular weekend visitation per our custody arrangement. I was at my office just over an hour before I was supposed to pick up my son at the Greenville County Law Enforcement Center when Cassidy sent a cryptic message to me.

Her subject line was simply, "Visitation," and her message was about cancelling it for the weekend. Despite that our court order mandated that this was my weekend to see our son, Cassidy told me in her message that a Department of Social Services (DSS) caseworker had been trying to contact me and that I needed to talk with her prior to visitation that evening. I was stunned. Why would a DSS caseworker be trying to contact me? My ex-wife's message did not do much to explain as it simply read, "I cannot go into details, but she can answer any questions you may have." I immediately knew that Cassidy was not oblivious to what was going on and that she was most likely the source of this DSS involvement in the first place.

I called the DSS caseworker named in Cassidy's email to find out what in the world was going on. She began explaining that there had been an abuse allegation leveled at me but that she could not go into details on the phone. I was completely numb. Though the caseworker would not reveal that Cassidy was the one who filed the report, I had no doubt in my mind. It was pretty clear to me what was going on. The family-court relocation case was not going well for Cassidy and her new husband, and now she had resorted to accusing me of being a child abuser.

The entire nasty affair that I thought was over at the end of 2013 had now become even nastier. It was a whole new ballgame after that call with the Department of Social Services.

CHAPTER 11

ABUSING THE CRIMINAL JUSTICE SYSTEM

I told the DSS agent that I knew the allegations were lodged by my ex-wife, and I began to give her some background on the years-long custody battle and Cassidy's newfound desire to leave the state with her new husband. I told her that I had no intentions of meeting with her and that she could direct any further questions or inquiries to my attorney. I was not about to bring a DSS agent to my place of work to interrogate me about allegations that my ex-wife had clearly fabricated to try and win a family-court relocation case. Both my attorney, Vanessa, and I agreed that we had no intentions of not following the normal visitation schedule and that Cassidy could not unilaterally cancel a visit because she decided to get down and dirty with false allegations.

Of course, Cassidy claimed that, due to the DSS investigation that she would not admit she had filed, she could not possibly bring my son to visitation. Vanessa and I agreed that I would go to the LEC, bring a witness with me, and then if Cassidy was a no-show, we would file a contempt motion in family court for violating the court order. So, as scheduled, I arrived at the Greenville County LEC that evening at 6pm with my friend, Paul Howell, as a witness. We waited for 20 minutes and called Cassidy again to remind her of visitation. Once it was clear she would be a no-show for visitation, I asked Paul to write a statement for use in the contempt action, and I noted the date and time for the court record.

With Cassidy filing allegations with DSS and now skipping visitation, I knew that any promise I held that 2014 would be the year of a new normalcy was shattered. As it would turn out, 2014 would be the worst year to date in my battle to be an active dad.

The following week, once my attorney had finally spoken at length with the DSS caseworker assigned to our case, we learned the nature of the allegations. We received confirmation that Cassidy was, in fact, the one who made the report. Cassidy was accusing me of sexual abuse of our then two-year-old son (he would turn three in June). She claimed that he had been sexually acting out around her and her husband and that she believed it was because I was teaching him sexual acts. When I learned of this, I was beyond livid. There is absolutely nothing worse to be accused of than being a child molester. I would much rather have been accused of murder than of molesting an innocent child, especially my own flesh and blood. That Cassidy would go to such an extreme to try and win a family-court case was, in my mind, cold-blooded and calculated.

While her blood may have been cold, mine was boiling. I can honestly say that it took every ounce of restraint that I could muster not to get into my car, drive to Cassidy's and her husband's house, and settle this matter of honor in the old-fashioned way. I had to be talked down by both of my lawyers and my pastor because I was fit to be tied. This was the last straw. I had taken nearly every abuse allegation imaginable from Cassidy and her family over the past three years, but this was a new low. There would be no turning back at this point. I would fight her until she could never make these allegations again.

My attorney filed a motion for emergency placement of my son away from Cassidy prior to any DSS investigation. Standard DSS procedures remove the child from the parent being accused of abuse—in this case, me—but Vanessa and I were convinced that this entire episode was Cassidy's attempt to relocate to Texas despite the lack of support she had for a family-court relocation case. As such, we told the family-court judge handling the emergency protective custody (EPC) hearing that we believed Cassidy was coaching my son to try and fabricate a sexual-abuse case against me for purposes of relocation and that my son needed to be equally quarantined from his mother leading up to the DSS abuse investigation. The judge seemed to agree, and my son was placed in my parents' custody on a temporary basis. Vanessa and I viewed this as a tremendous victory. Cassidy had made the allegations, and the judge agreed with us that leaving our son with her may prejudice a fair investigation of the claims.

The DSS scheduled a forensic interview at a local sexual abuse center so that a sexual psychologist could interview my son and determine if there were, in fact, any signs of my son being sexually molested. At the time when my mother and I showed up with my son the morning of the interview, the Mauldin City Police was there, the DSS was there, and Cassidy and her family had come to be there for the interview even though they were not supposed to be there.

As my son was taken into an interview room, the Mauldin City police detective asked if he could speak with me for a few minutes. He and I went into a holding room, and he began to explain that neither Cassidy nor I were supposed to be there for the interview. As such, he said, they would reschedule the interview for later in the week and that my mother could bring him alone.

The detective and I talked for a while about the history of the case and all of Cassidy's past allegations in family court before we got up to leave. He seemed sympathetic and understanding as he had become familiar with the three-year custody battle and all of the allegations my ex-wife had made for years in an attempt to gain custody and financial support. He told me that, if my son's interview was clear, he would move to charge Cassidy with filing a false police report.

The detective's pledge gave me hope. I was confident that my son's interview would conclusively prove that he had not been sexually abused and certainly not by me. I took him at his word that Cassidy would finally be held to some account for the constant claims she had made against me in our years-long custody struggle. For years, she had made every manner of vile accusation, all in a pretty obvious attempt to ensure that my son would no longer have a relationship with his father. Such selfishness was infuriating to me more for what it did to my son than for what it did to me.

As expected, when the forensic interview reports were completed, they concluded that there was no evidence that my son had been sexually abused and that he had made no such statement during the interviews. Almost immediately after the forensic interview findings were reported, Social Services dismissed the case as "unfounded." Just as with all the other allegations Cassidy had lodged against me over the past three years, these, too, were proven to be unsubstantiated. The damage was done, however, and an already extremely difficult co-parenting arrangement was rendered nearly impossible.

Interestingly, shortly after Cassidy's allegations against me were deemed unfounded, her need to immediately leave the state was alleviated. Cassidy informed her counsel and mine that her husband had been reassigned to Shaw Air Force Base near Sumter, South Carolina. While Sumter is a nearly three-hour drive from the Upstate where we all lived, it was significantly closer than Abilene, Texas. Even after making sexual-abuse allegations, my former wife agreed to a consent order of joint custody with essentially equal physical custody now that she was staying in the state. I was thrilled that I would share a week-on/week-off visitation arrangement with Cassidy. We would meet mid-way to exchange our son on Sundays, but I was also stunned that she would agree to joint custody within weeks of making sexual-abuse allegations. To me, that tipped her hand and showed that she never truly believed her own assertions.

With the new week-on/week-off arrangement in place, Cassidy and I also agreed to take co-parenting classes with a local psychologist who specializes in childhood development. Our respective attorneys and the court believed that we needed third-party help to rebuild some semblance of trust and a working relationship after the allegations that had been made. While any remaining trust I had in Cassidy was lost with the sexual-abuse claims, I agreed to the co-parenting therapy provision of our new custody arrangement because something had to help. Clearly, we were not going to be able to resolve our differences on our own anymore.

During the summer after the allegations were made, my sweet son turned three, and I was enjoying more time with him than at any point since he had been born. The summer of 2014 was a sweet time of my son finding some stability and being able to see both sides of his family with regularity. I felt like he was beginning to settle into a stable routine that gave him the security he had been denied since Cassidy's and my separation in July of 2011. With Cassidy's outrageous allegations unfounded and with a co-parenting therapist in the picture, I believed that the worst was now behind us.

That was until I got another message from Cassidy on August 5, 2014 that read,

Josh,

I wanted to thank you for your cooperation in doing what's best for [our son] as we planned to relocate to Shaw AFB. John and I were thankful for your willingness to meet us between Shaw AFB and Greenville to exchange [our son].

Due to unforeseen circumstances, John has been diverted to Texas and the station at Shaw AFB is not available due to an error on the Air Force's behalf. John will be on leave soon and will be back in the state; we would like to meet with you to discuss potential visitation arrangements. We think it is in [our son's] best interest to work together amicably regarding the situation. Although still on the diversion list, John is currently assigned to Dyess AFB, Texas. We wanted to keep you informed of things on our end and look forward to working with you on a visitation schedule that would benefit [our son]. When would be a good time to meet and discuss things?

Thank you again for working with us.

Sincerely,
Cassidy Hatfield

I was floored when I received this message about an hour before midnight. The same circumstances that preceded Cassidy's sexual-abuse allegations had now returned. The same need to leave the state that I believe prompted the proceedings around Easter was now pressing again, and I was very concerned. I was convinced that Cassidy's sexual-abuse allegations against me were absolutely motivated by her need to leave the state with her new husband. The newfound cooperation that had existed during the summer of 2014 seemed to be rooted in the fact that she and John were going to be staying in the state at Shaw Air Force Base. Now that Shaw was off the table, I was deeply concerned that sexual-abuse allegations may be back on the table.

CHAPTER 12

FROM DAD TO DEFENDANT

I never agreed to meet with Cassidy after her email on August 5th. After all that had happened between us since she left our marriage in July of 2011, I did not feel comfortable sitting down over a cup of coffee to hammer out details of a relocation custody arrangement with her and her husband. Not to mention that I honestly had no intentions of supporting her renewed request to take our toddler son halfway across America to live on an Air Force base with a man I knew little about and to whom she had only been married for a matter of months. My attorney and I responded that we would, again, not support any attempt to alter the joint-custody agreement that was put into place after Cassidy's sexual-abuse allegations against me were dismissed in the spring. We did not believe it was good for my son's stability and relationship with his family to again change his visitation schedule because Cassidy and her husband had another relocation issue.

As far as I was concerned, the ball was now in Cassidy's court as to what she needed to do to arrange travel to visit our son in South Carolina—not take our son to Texas. That was the position we took from a family-court perspective. We had no intentions of agreeing to any changes to the joint-custody agreement voluntarily. I assumed that was case closed and that Cassidy and John would have to work out something on their own as the sexual-abuse allegation had been dismissed, and joint custody had been put into place in the aftermath of that failed attempt. It honestly never crossed my mind that she could successfully dip into that well twice by making the same allegations with any credibility. I was wrong.

By late summer, we were informed that Cassidy's relocation motion would go before the Greenville County Family Court in October. There would be a hearing before a family-court judge who would have to rule on whether or not Cassidy would be granted permission to, as primary legal custodian, take our son across state lines. While Cassidy and I shared physical custody of our son after her first sexual-abuse allegations, the agreement still gave her the designation of primary legal custodian. It is incredibly hard as a father in South Carolina—even when the merits of a case seemingly recommended it—to gain primary legal custody. Vanessa and I felt confident that the court would not allow Cassidy to leave the state, primary legal custodian or not, after the allegations she had made earlier in the year and her voluntary agreement to go to joint physical custody shortly after making those allegations. What bolstered our confidence was that the guardian ad litem assigned to our case did not seem to support or recommend the relocation motion.

As September rolled along, the South Carolina election season was heating up. By virtue of my daily radio program and the associated policy foundation that I chair to engage in South Carolina's issues, I was busier than normal. In addition to my work as a commercial banker and dealing with the ongoing custody issues with Cassidy and her husband, I was campaigning around the state with a number of candidates for U.S.

Congress in support of South Carolina Governor Nikki Haley's reelection. My team and I hosted BBQs, cocktail receptions, and meet-and-greets for some of our state's most visible conservative leaders, and we were optimistic that our efforts would help bolster the Republican ticket in November.

One of the last two big public events we planned to host as part of the 2014 election cycle was a "Rule of Law Townhall and BBQ" in Spartanburg, featuring U.S. Congressmen Trey Gowdy and Mick Mulvaney from the fourth and fifth congressional districts of South Carolina, respectively. Both Trey and Mick had become friends during their time in Congress as they had been regular guests on my radio program and at our policy foundation's public dinners and receptions. I strongly supported their congressional reelections. Thus, we decided to hold a joint townhall BBQ for them on Thursday evening, September 25th. We had about 150 invited guests at this white-tablecloth, BBQ dinner that was going to be served on a golf course with the two congressmen and me conducting a townhall meeting on a portable stage placed among the tables. It was a wonderful evening full of energy and promise. It was a welcome distraction from the continued custody issues that were swirling around my family. That was the last night of calm before the storm would take a turn for the worst.

I was still exuberant the next morning—Friday, September 26th—after the successful event my team had pulled off in Spartanburg the night before. I was also buoyed by the fact that South Carolina Governor Nikki Haley had just nominated me to serve as a member of the state's Pardon, Probation, and Parole Board on the recommendation of my friend, Congressman Gowdy. It seemed that my career both in banking and politics was still moving along despite the constant struggle that my personal life had become. I was hopeful that I would be able to pursue my calling and passion while fighting to be a father to my little boy. On that Friday morning, I was optimistic despite the coming custody hearing, and I was scheduled to spend the weekend with my little boy as my week of visitation was set to commence at 6pm that evening.

Shortly before noon on that morning filled with optimism, I received a phone call from a Detective Briana Valentino of the Greenville City Police. The detective asked if I had some time to talk with her about a police report my wife had filed on Wednesday evening in which she claimed that I had abused our son. I had a mid-week visit on Wednesday evening for three hours (our standard off-week visit while the other parent had their week of visitation), and it appeared that Cassidy had come back to the Greenville County Law Enforcement Center shortly after I had dropped of my son to her to file a police report against me. The claim was, once again, sexual abuse.

I actually laughed at the detective. I told her that this was not my first rodeo with Cassidy's outrageous allegations, and I told her about the recent case back in the spring in which my former wife had gone to the Police Department of the City of Mauldin, a town just outside Greenville, to make the same sexual-abuse allegations when she needed to relocate out of South Carolina. I explained to Detective Valentino that the same preconditions that preceded the last round of sexual-abuse allegations existed again; Cassidy needed to leave South Carolina to join her new husband in Texas, and she wanted to take our son with her. I told the detective that I did not plan to meet with her on these allegations because there was no merit to the claims. Instead, I asked her to call my attorney, Vanessa, to discuss whatever Cassidy had told her and to clear the air on another set of false allegations.

I was a bit shaken by the call from the Greenville Detective but was not too worried. I assumed that, once Detective Valentino reviewed the file and Cassidy's history, this report—like the previous one—would be thrown out. When I called to tell Vanessa that I needed her to speak with this detective, she was actually excited. She felt that Cassidy's second round of allegations in less than six months, all coinciding with a pending relocation motion, would work in our favor at winning primary legal custody of my son and putting an end to this nightmare once and for all. She felt that Cassidy may have overplayed her hand and that this may be the final straw for the family court to finally put a stop to her serial allegations and constant stream of lawsuits. I tended to agree.

The thing that most bothered me about the call from the detective was that Cassidy used it as another excuse to skip court-ordered visitation. Just as she had done in the spring, Cassidy refused to bring my son to the LEC for visitation exchange, and just as I had done before, I went to the LEC with a witness to document that she skipped visitation and was in violation of our court order. This time, I even went into the LEC lobby and filed a police report with the Greenville County Sherriff's Office to note that she had skipped visitation. I wanted more than my and a friend's affidavits this time around. I wanted an official report that she was, yet again, flouting the family court and imposing her will against our custody order. Despite my best efforts, Cassidy never came that evening and, in fact, refused to let me see my son at any point during what was supposed to be my week for visitation.

We ended up back in court for yet another Emergency Protective Custody (EPC) hearing, and Vanessa was once again prepared to recommend that my mother and/or brother serve as temporary custodians until this latest round of insanity could be unraveled. As before, the allegations leveled against me by my former wife meant that my son would not be placed in my care, but—also as before—the court was skeptical about my ex-wife's constant stream of allegations and did not support placing my son with her, either. My counsel and I believed that the court would, once again, place my son with my family as a stop-gap measure until we could debunk Cassidy's outrageous claims. The protestations of Cassidy's attorney, however, were such that the judge made a decision that I hoped would never come. She took my son from every member of both sides of his family and placed him in the custody of the Department of Social Services. My son was going to a foster home.

I was outraged. For four years, my son had been used as a weapon against me by my ex-wife, and he was beginning to show the emotional scars of such abuse. Because of the constant back-and-forth custody arrangements—which resulted from Cassidy's constant abuse allegations, DSS reports, police reports, etc.—my son was already struggling with significant separation anxiety. The last thing he needed was to be further removed from any semblance of security in his life by being placed into a foster home by protective services. Vanessa and I made every appeal we could to keep our son out of foster care, but everything we recommended was shot down by Cassidy's attorney, and the judge was unwilling to do alternative placement without both parties agreeing. There was nothing we could do; my son would be in foster care without access to his family until this nightmare could be sorted out... again.

I went home the evening of the hearing, heartbroken for my son. I was so very worried about what he must have been going through, where he may have been, and with whom he might be staying. A dear friend of mine who is involved in many local ministries and served as a local

Chick-Fil-A regional marketing director came to my aide. She had been present for all of the hearings, and she had great contacts in the foster care community because so many of her friends were, themselves, foster parents. Almost immediately after my son was taken into DSS custody, she got to work to figure out where he was and if he was okay. It took us about 24 hours to find out that he was, on a temporary basis, being housed in a Miracle Hill group home until a foster family could be assigned. While it was devastating to hear that my son was in a group home with complete strangers, there was some relief in the fact that the home was run by Miracle Hill, a local Christian relief ministry with which I had some relationship.

My friend informed me that my son was doing as well as could be expected and was being treated very kindly by the team at Miracle Hill. She also told me that it seemed he would be moving out of the group home soon as he had been assigned to a foster family who had a little girl roughly my son's age. I was grateful that he was being taken care of by a Christian ministry that partnered with our state's DSS, but there is nothing that gives a parent any real comfort when his or her child is in state custody and does not even know where his or her child is sleeping at night. For me, this was pure hell. Not knowing where my son was living was the most helpless and difficult experience I had ever felt.

At the same time that my family and I were reeling over the fact that my son had been taken into DSS custody, I had to fend-off continued allegations from Cassidy. During my son's early days in foster care, he was, once again, scheduled to go to a local forensic interview center to be interviewed for potential signs of sexual abuse, the same stuff he had to endure just six months earlier when Cassidy played the sexual-abuse card the first time. My son had to endure not one but two separate interviews at the request of the Greenville City Police detective, Briana Valentino, with whom I had spoken the day after my BBQ in Spartanburg with our Upstate Congressional Delegation. This detective seemed determined to find a way to make a case against me despite all the evidence that completely contradicted Cassidy's claims.

The first forensic interview of this cycle came back, unsurprisingly, without any indication of sexual abuse. My son had made no disclosures of abuse, and there was nothing that supported Cassidy's accusations. Because the first one was clear, the detective asked for a second interview, which was actually his third in six months. I was amazed; it was as if the Greenville City Police Department was aiding my ex-wife in her witch hunt for something to use against me in her relocation case. What had started as a family-court case had now morphed into a criminal prosecution against me, and all I wanted was to be an active and involved father to my son who had been taken from me shortly after birth.

Between the first and second forensic interviews at the child advocacy center, Detective Valentino called me to setup a time for me to come down to the Law Enforcement Center to discuss the case. Even though I knew that I had done nothing wrong, I decided not to go without a criminal defense attorney as it was obvious to me that this detective had some sort of agenda and wanted to make Cassidy's claims stick. I knew that I was not dealing with an objective, arbiter of the facts but rather a person who, for whatever reason, was emotionally invested in the case in favor of Cassidy and her allegations. I called the office of a local criminal defense attorney who had worked in the local district attorney's office to ask if I could retain his services in the event I was arrested over these false allegations and to go to the police interview with me.

After paying my retainer to this criminal defense attorney, I called back and setup a time for the two of us to meet with Detective Valentino to discuss the case she was trying to build against me. Shortly before the meeting at the law enforcement center, Vanessa's office got a transcript of the second forensic interview of my son. Again, it was totally clear; it showed nothing that would in any way support Cassidy's claims that my son was struggling with the after effects of sexual abuse and no indication that my son had ever been abused. I actually read through the transcripts of the interviews before my meeting with the detective, and I felt even more convinced that this meeting was nothing more than a last-ditch, desperate attempt by the detective to find some evidence to bolster her case. I certainly was not going to be any help to her cause.

When my criminal defense attorney and I arrived to meet with Detective Valentino, it was immediately adversarial. It was clear that she was grasping at straws, but it was also clear that she wanted to make this case stick somehow, for some reason. When she started discussing the forensic interviews, unaware that I had read the transcript, I began quoting from the transcript about what had been said. She seemed shocked and a little shaken that I already knew the interviews were clear and that nothing supported Cassidy's claims. She kept probing for information and was increasingly frustrated that I was not giving her anything to work with to build a circumstantial case. Finally, after we talked for half an hour, she asked my attorney and me if I would take a polygraph test. Before I could even think about agreeing, my criminal defense attorney butted in and told her no. I was a little shocked.

As we walked out, my attorney told me that the reason he said no to the polygraph was that he has watched this play out too many times in which the police have nothing else to work with, so they will talk someone into a polygraph and then work to make them as nervous as possible and try to force them to make a deal. He felt like this particular detective was determined to make an issue out of Cassidy's allegations and that giving her any opening would prolong the process of getting these ludicrous allegations tossed out. One additional thing that made him nervous—any, by extension, me—was that the detective would not rule out yet another forensic interview with my son by the same center that had already interviewed him twice in this present round of allegations and once six months prior when Cassidy went to the Mauldin City Police to launch unfounded allegations. This detective was fishing, it seemed, and I had no idea why.

My attorney said that he would follow up with the detective and be sure that she understood that these allegations were nothing new, that they had been found false just six months prior, and that all of this was taking place in the context of a four-year custody battle that began when my wife left our marriage in the summer of 2011. He also conveyed to the detective that if, God forbid, she decided to issue a warrant for my arrest, we would cooperate in the sense that I would go down to the LEC and turn myself in. The last thing we wanted was to make a public spectacle out of an already horrible situation that had gotten wildly out of hand.

Honestly, the fact that we even had to discuss the possibility of turning myself in if a warrant was issued for my arrest was unnerving. I could not believe that this had gone so far. In six months, there had been a total of three forensic interviews conducted with my child and not a single statement pointed to sexual abuse while Cassidy's allegations several months earlier had been deemed by DSS as unfounded. Another municipality (Mauldin) had investigated and dismissed the same allegations six months prior, and DSS had unfounded the case. All of that seemed to suggest that this latest round of character assassination should have ended much more quickly than it had. I was beginning to get pretty worried.

By mid-October, the entire situation had gone from bad to worse. While the forensic interviews were all clear, the DSS still had to conduct its full investigation into the claims leveled against me, including conducting interviews with family members. This meant that my son had to stay in foster care until the DSS investigation was completed and the allegations, yet again, determined to be unfounded. I was worried sick about my son, who was days into his forced exile by the family court. No one in my family had spoken with him, seen him, or been given any kind of report on how he was doing. That is not a position that any responsible parent should ever be placed in, yet that was exactly where I was for days, wondering where my little boy was living and with whom.

Before this outrage began, my radio and policy foundation team and I had already begun making plans to be part of the upcoming South Carolina Republican Presidential Primary, which would begin in earnest in 2015. We had decided to partner with a friend of mine from Spartanburg, Karen Floyd, past chairman of the South Carolina Republican Party, to host the presidential candidates for a series of forums. The first of these forums was scheduled for Saturday, October 11th, at Spartanburg Methodist College with Texas U.S. Senator Ted Cruz. I would moderate a panel of local media personalities that would interview the Senator on stage before a live audience on Saturday, and my policy foundation would then join the Spartanburg GOP in hosting Senator Cruz for an ice cream social on Sunday afternoon to round out the Senator's weekend visit to South Carolina.

By the time these events actually rolled around, I was dealing with the reality that my son was in state custody, my wife had—for the second time in six months—accused me of abusing my own son, and the family court was considering whether or not to allow her to take our son to Texas. Needless to say, I was not in a frame of mind to engage in the opening salvos of the presidential primary, yet I had little choice. Few people beyond my immediate family and close friends even knew that any of this was happening, and I could not start canceling events that had been in the works for weeks and even months. As I introduced Senator Cruz at our last event on Sunday afternoon, my mind kept drifting toward my son. I could not stop worrying about how he was doing and how hard it was for him to be away from his family.

Being that I am a commercial banker as well as a political activist and talk-radio host, I have federal holidays off. The day after our ice-cream social was Monday, October 13th; in 2014, that day was Columbus Day. The bank was closed, and I had no public events that I was scheduled to be part of related to anything political. The only thing on my schedule for Monday was to sit at home, think and pray for my son and about the situation, and then host my daily radio program across town that evening at 5pm. Monday was hard. It had rained almost all weekend, and the Sunday downpours had carried over into Monday. The overcast skies, cooling October temperatures, and the steady sprinkle of rain all matched my mood. Despite the whirlwind of exciting events over the weekend, I was deeply depressed by what had happened with my son and that the allegations against were still hanging over my head.

CHAPTER 13

MY DAY THAT WILL LIVE IN
INFAMY

Tuesday, October 14th, 2014, is a day that will haunt me all the days of my life. The same rain that had drizzled all day Monday was now pouring on Tuesday morning. With Columbus Day over, banks were reopened, and schools were back in session. I left early for the office, hoping that I could focus on the mountains of work on my desk with the storm raging around me. I worked as diligently as I could that morning, but I could not help but wonder whether or not the Greenville City Police was finally ready to toss Cassidy's false allegations so that we could expedite my son's return home. Because Cassidy had skipped my last visitation and because the court had put my son in foster care, it had been over two weeks since I had seen my son. Something had to give, and this situation needed to be resolved—most importantly for my son but for all of us involved.

After working for a few hours, I decided to walk across the parking lot from my office for a long-delayed haircut, hoping that the time out of the office would calm my nerves and clear my head. I stepped out into the driving rain for the three-minute jaunt across the saturated parking lot for what I assumed would be a routine, 30-minute hair appointment.

As I stepped in the front lobby to sign in and await my stylist, my phone began to ring in my back pants pocket. I almost didn't pull it out to answer it, but I was expecting a call from Vanessa's paralegal, and I was hopeful that today would be the day when the good news came.

When I looked down at the screen of my iPhone, I saw "DETECTIVE VALENTINO" coming across my call screen. My immediate reaction was not necessarily negative as I thought it was very likely that she was calling to say that the department had decided, like the Mauldin City Police and the DSS just months ago, that Cassidy's claims had been deemed unfounded. I stepped back from the counter to catch the call and picked up just before it was set to go to voicemail. When I answered, the detective asked, "Mr. Kimbrell?"

I replied, "This is him. How may I help you?"

She replied, "I wanted to let you know that I just issued a warrant for your arrest, and you agreed to work with us."

I replied that I would and asked her what we needed to do now.

"Please plan on coming down to the law enforcement center around 1pm today."

With that, the call and, seemingly, my world ended.

To this day, I do not remember what, if anything, I said to the receptionist at the salon. I remember only walking back across the parking lot without so much as popping open my umbrella. I could not believe this. These were false allegations, there was absolutely no evidence to back them up, and Cassidy's credibility was severely dented after having so many of her past allegations deemed unfounded and tossed aside. How a four-year custody war could result in an innocent father getting arrested because his ex-wife wanted to take the child out of state was beyond me. I could not fathom how this had happened. I remember only calling my mother to tell her that I was getting ready to go downtown to turn myself in and the stunned silence that punctuated the moment. Her response was simple. "Your dad and I will meet you there." My next two calls were to attorneys, one to Vanessa to tell her that our family-court case had now become criminal and the other to my criminal defense attorney to ask him to meet me at the LEC.

The call came at shortly before 11am that morning, meaning that I had about two hours to get ready to… be arrested. I had no idea how to deal with this; my emotions ran the gambit. I had never even been issued a speeding ticket, much less been arrested for anything. Over those next two hours, my mind was reeling. I assumed that my life was basically over. I believed that I would never see my son again, that my career was certainly over, and that I may end up in a prison for a crime I did not commit. When I finally got on the phone with my criminal attorney's paralegal, she assured me that this would just be a booking and that I would just go down to the law enforcement center, be finger-printed, be formally charged, and then be released until we could get this sorted out in court. None of that sounded okay, but at least it seemed like I may get to come back to my own bed that evening.

Finally, 20 minutes before 1pm, I met my family outside my apartment to ride with them to be formally arrested. For what? I did not know. On the advice of counsel, I dressed as casually as I could because I was told not to bring my wallet, personal items, or anything valuable. I ended up wearing a worn pair of jeans, an old worn-out pair of Sperry topsiders, a t-shirt, and a light Clemson sweater-jacket over the shirt. When I climbed into the back of my family's SUV, my heart was racing, and my feet felt like cement. I was truly terrified that I was being rail-roaded for no other reason than that I refused to give up on my own son.

`JOSH KIMBRELL`

I was going to be prosecuted for trying to be a parent who didn't abandon his own child.

Once we arrived at the law enforcement center, I met my pastor, Dr. Mike Hamlet, and my defense attorney in the front lobby. Once my attorney arrived, he walked over to the reception counter to ask for Detective Valentino to inform her that his client had arrived to turn himself in for... something. Neither my attorney nor I knew what the formal charge was even as we were walking in the door. The detective did not bother mentioning it to me when she called a few hours earlier, and she had not even conveyed that to my attorney. When the detective finally arrived in the lobby, she and another officer asked my attorney and me to come with them as they led us out the front door and back out into the parking lot. I said goodbye to my family and my pastor and told them that I planned on seeing them in a few hours. That was not to be.

As we walked down a sidewalk toward the booking and processing center inside the Greenville County Detention Center, which is right next door to the law enforcement center, my defense attorney asked the detective what the charge was against me. Valentino quickly replied, "Criminal sexual conduct with minor under the age of 11 in the first degree,"

My attorney responded, "Based on what evidence?"

The detective's reply was equally rapid and forceful. "The mother's polygraph, the child's forensic interviews, and the child's medical records."

I am not an attorney, so even in that moment, I did not understand the severity of the charge being leveled against me, but I certainly didn't think it sounded good. Beyond that, I was stunned that this Greenville City Police detective was citing my child's medical records and forensic

— 134 —

interviews as the primary reasons for my arrest. My family law attorney, Vanessa, had already reviewed the forensic transcripts and subpoenaed my child's medical records; all were squeaky clean. None of that seemed to faze this detective, who had clearly planned on arresting me from the moment we first spoke.

What I did not know at the time but later learned from a deputy district attorney who decided to run for the South Carolina State Senate in the 2016 GOP Primary and called me for my help was that the district attorney's office had already declined to prosecute prior to the detective arresting me. In South Carolina, we call our district attorneys *solicitors*, and their assistants are called *deputy solicitors*. What this one particular deputy solicitor told me over a year later was that the detective called the solicitor's office and asked the chief sex crimes prosecutor what she thought about my case. She had, apparently, told the detective that the solicitor's office would not prosecute the case based on lack of evidence.

I didn't know that on October 14, 2014—not that it mattered much. The detective had found a gullible magistrate unfamiliar with her conversation with the solicitor's office to sign off on the warrant. I suppose her attitude was that, even if the solicitor's office didn't plan to prosecute the case, she would still take out a warrant against me. And so she did. Now, I was walking toward the county jail with an incredulous attorney and a detective who clearly had some agenda.

As we arrived at the perimeter fence around the booking area of the detention center, I was formally read my Miranda rights and cuffed by a uniformed officer who was clearly agitated. My attorney told me that he would talk to me inside, and I was separated from both him and Detective Valentino as I was led into the intake and bookings area of the jailhouse. As we walked through the fenced parking lot with me in handcuffs, this angry officer who had cuffed me began yelling at me and telling me what I pervert I was for what I did. He started openly mocking me for hosting a conservative political talk radio program on a station affiliated with a Christian radio network and calling me a monster. It was clear that he believed that, even without a trial, I was already "guilty until proven innocent."

Being cuffed, yelled at by a uniformed Greenville City police officer, and locked into a holding room had taken its psychological toll. I was in shock. It was all like a nightmare, and I had to remind myself that I was not asleep. I was in jail. IN JAIL. I had never had any more interaction with local police than seeing them at football games and in their patrol cars, yet I was now the object of their wrath, a man charged with a first-degree felony sex charge for allegedly molesting a toddler. None of these other officers knew the true story that the toddler in question was my own son, that my accuser was my former wife, and that we had been embroiled in a four-year custody fight. All they knew was that I was in the clink for being a child molester and that my victim was a toddler. Even by jail standards, I was viewed as evil and unredeemable. Every officer treated me as such, and I was afforded the most disrespectful and barbaric treatment allowable under law.

Shortly after being locked in a holding room until I could be processed and booked, I was allowed to take a phone call from my criminal defense attorney. It was not good news. He was not allowed in where I was because he told me that the charges filed against me carried a life sentence. There was no way that he could get me out on bail for at least 24 hours, and I was definitely going to be spending the night in jail. I was devastated. My family was waiting to take me back to my apartment, and now, I was being locked in the Greenville County Detention Center unexpectedly and without any advance notice or time to prepare. Even worse, the charges against me carried a penalty of life imprisonment without the possibility of parole. I still could not believe that a detective could get a warrant without any evidence, much less throw the book at me with charges that carried a life sentence in the state penitentiary.

After being fingerprinted and having my mugshot taken, I was taken to another holding room where I was forced to strip off my clothes in front of a corrections officer. I was then issued a standard orange jumpsuit, handed a dirty blanket and a small container with toiletries, and told to follow yet another corrections officer to where I would be housed. The corrections officer who supervised my changing into the jumpsuit asked me what I was in for, and I told him that my former wife had accused me of sexually abusing our son in a custody battle. His facial expression betrayed the first hint of empathy that I had gotten from anyone since I set foot behind the fence earlier in the day. He told me that I should not tell any of the other inmates what I had been arrested for because they might be violent toward me as an accused child molester. He also told me that I would "probably" be okay because I was being housed in a cell block with other people arrested for sex-crimes allegations.

I wanted to break down and sob, but I refused to show weakness in front of the corrections officers and, especially, the other inmates. So, I grabbed my blanket, my thin standard-issue mattress, and my toiletries bag and followed a corrections officer through a labyrinth of metal doors, heavy gates, and concrete hallways and staircases until I came to "O dorm," the place where sex offenders were housed. I was led into the cell block, assigned a bunk bed, and the door was closed and locked behind me. There were about 10 other men in this cell block, none of whom spoke to me upon arrival. There were five cell rooms that opened into a common area with a bolted-down, metal picnic table and a common-area shower with no curtain. There were two men per cell room, and each room had bars on them. The cell block was largely windowless, save a small opening in the heavy metal door. It was the closest thing to hell I had ever experienced on earth.

When I walked into the cell where I would be sleeping on the top bunk, a Bible was laying on the metal frame where I was to lay my mattress. It was left there by my new bunkmate who, for sport, had been ordering copies of the Bible so that he could rip the pages out and flush them down the toilet. Because I came to jail with absolutely nothing, I asked the man if I could keep this copy to myself, to which he agreed. That worn paperback Bible would become my anchor during the toughest trial of my life as I read it by day and slept on it at night. The detention center would not provide a pillow for us as that was considered a potential suicide weapon, so we either had to sleep with our head against the metal railing or on our folded hands. I used the Bible as my pillow while sleeping. In part, I slept on it for some degree of comfort but also so that no one could steal it from me. During the day, I tried to keep to myself and read from it on my bunk.

I was locked in my cell around 2pm that Tuesday afternoon, terrified and very alone. By that evening, I did manage to introduce myself to the man in the bunk below me and a few of the other men living in the rooms next to mine. What struck me was the fact that virtually everyone in my cell block was very young, mid-20s to late-30s. What also struck me and scared me deeply was how long virtually every one of these inmates had been jailed awaiting a jury trial. Most could not post bond even if they could get a bond hearing before the Court of General Sessions, which handled class-I felony charges. Most of the men living in my dorm had been in the detention center for at least nine months and some for well over a year. Because I never expected to see an overnight stay in jail, the prospect of staying for months or years was truly disheartening.

I largely tried to keep to myself during that first day in the detention center. I had never been behind bars even for a visit, much less spent time around men who were locked up for sex crimes—in the case of at least one of the people on my cell block, sexual assault and homicide. Nevertheless, I needed to find a way to call out and reconnect with my family. Contrary to popular belief, I was not afforded "one phone call," and no one even told me how to log into the pay phone attached to one of the concrete walls in my cell block, much less how to pay for time on the phone when I came into the detention center without my wallet and without any money. I had not been planning on spending the night. As such, my conversing with my cellmate was a necessity; he knew how to use the phone, and he had a log-on prepaid card.

Tony was the name of the man with whom I would share a jail cell at that time. He was also the only person who helped me survive those days of incarceration and isolation. I have no way of knowing whether or not Tony was guilty of the allegations against him. For obvious reasons, I no longer hold the conviction that anyone the police arrests is probably guilty. My eyes have been opened to how easy it actually is to be arrested in America. Regardless of Tony's innocence or guilt, he helped me learn how to survive in confinement, primarily by teaching me how to get on the phone to call my family and my lawyers. I was afraid going in that I may need to have my parents' and Vanessa's phone numbers handy… in case I was detained. Because I could carry nothing with me, I wrote their names and numbers on my left arm with an ink pin on the way to the LEC the afternoon of my arrest. After being stripped of everything I was wearing and being put into an orange jumpsuit, I was happy that I had thought of it.

The first call to my family was heart wrenching. I called my mom's cell number, and she was greatly shaken that I had been detained and that it did not look like I was going to be getting out anytime soon. She tried to be optimistic, but because I had been charged with a class-A felony that carried a life sentence, a magistrate court could not grant to me a bond hearing as they can with lesser charges. I was stunned that a magistrate judge could sign an arrest warrant for a class-A felony, thus placing an accused person in jail but that they were unable to grant a bond hearing. That seems inconsistent to me. Nevertheless, that was the way the bond-hearing process worked, and I would have to wait until the South Carolina Court of General Sessions was back in session so that my criminal defense attorney could try to secure a bond amount for me to get bonded out of jail while awaiting my trial.

My mom told me that she had been working through my cellphone trying to call people who might be able to help, including a friend of mine who was currently serving South Carolina in Congress. What neither my mom nor I knew was that the conversations we were having over the detention center's phone line were being recorded. As soon as the jailers heard me talking with my mother about her calling a member of Congress, unbeknownst to me at the time, they called his chief of staff. All of this was happening within hours of my being arrested, and it was becoming pretty heated outside the walls of the detention center, and I was completely disconnected. I was sealed off from the world.

— 140 —

Even though I had hired a criminal defense attorney to handle my case, I did not have much of a relationship with him other than sitting through the interview with Detective Valentino with him. He was working on the bond issue, and he was in touch with my family, but I did not have very much interaction with him during my time in the detention center. I was just hoping that he would come and see me in jail and give me some idea about what was happening and what we were going to do to rectify this wrong. Finally, at around 8pm that first evening, a corrections officer came over the intercom system in my cell block and told me that I had a "pro-v." That means, "professional, or attorney, visit." It was about time, I thought, considering I had been sitting on my cot for six hours with no idea what was happening. Maybe I would, somehow, still get out tonight?

I was led down the hallway to the visitation gallery, hoping that my criminal defense attorney had come to give me some good news. When I arrived, it was my friend and family lawyer, Vanessa, who had come to check on me. Even though she was not my criminal defense attorney, her credentials as an attorney got her into the visitation gallery. Just seeing a friendly face was a sight for sore eyes. The six hours I had spent in jail seemed like days already, and the fact that Vanessa came to see me was very moving. She had been coordinating with my family and people associated with my radio program so that they would know how to respond. She also coordinated with my criminal attorney about bonding me out. Despite everyone's efforts, it seemed like it would be several days before I would get out of jail. I needed to mentally prepare for several days in jail before any sort of bond hearing could be had.

The next day, October 15th, was when all hell broke loose publically. I figured that, at some point, news that a local conservative talk radio host was in jail would make its way into the public spotlight. How bad it would be when the news did break was the part for which I was unprepared. As I was still sitting in my jail cell, trying to read the Bible and keep to myself, the local NBC affiliate's evening news broadcast came on the cellblock television set. I heard the voice of local anchor Michael Cogdill talking about the funeral of another local talk-radio host, an acquaintance who broadcasted on another station, who had died suddenly during the weekend prior. That news caught my attention, and I decided to walk out into the common area so that I could see the television. Moments after covering the funeral, the anchors began going over news of local arrests. Mine was at the top of the list.

The release from the Greenville Police was as close to a complete smear as an agency can legally engage in when someone is arrested but not convicted. The news anchors read the copy that read,

> An Upstate man who is the host of a conservative radio show on a Christian talk channel has been charged with a sex crime against a three-year old boy, according to arrest warrants. Josh Kimbrell, who is host of "Common Cents" on Christian Talk 660AM / 92.9FM, is charged with first-degree criminal sexual conduct with a minor under 11.
>
> According to the arrest warrant, Kimbrell, under the guise of a game, fondled the child and committed other sexual acts against the boy. Greenville Police said that Kimbrell was arrested Tuesday. He is being held without bond.

Kimbrell's Common Cents show airs weekdays at 5pm. He was born and raised in the Upstate and attending North Greenville University, according to his website. It says he is also chair of the Palmetto Conservative Alliance.

Recently, Kimbrell hosted Reps. Trey Gowdy and Mick Mulvaney at an outdoor barbecue event on September 25th titled "Restoring the Rule of Law." The radio station officials told WYFF News 4 that they have no comment at this time.

My blood was boiling as I watched this play out on television while I was sitting in jail with no way to respond. It seemed to me that the Greenville Police were trying to get out in front of the story by portraying me as guilty until proven innocent. The story did not report that the three-year old that I was accused of molesting was my own son or that the accuser was my former wife with whom I had been engaged in a four-year custody battle. The news stories were that a local talk-radio host who worked with members of Congress and served on the Governor's reelection campaign steering committee was arrested for being a child molester. An already horrible situation had now been made worse because it had now been made into a political story in addition to a custody battle gone wrong.

The way the story was broken to the state could not have been worse. I was portrayed as being arrested for molesting a three-year old like a pedophile who lurked behind a daycare. No mention was made on those evening broadcasts or by the Greenville Police that this was part of an ongoing custody dispute that an overzealous detective had helped to go nuclear.

As I sat there watching the news with my fellow inmates, my thoughts immediately turned to the advice of the officer in charge of my booking to keep sexual-abuse charges to myself. Even in prison, there's a code of ethics, and sexually molesting a child violates it. My blood ran cold. I was absolutely innocent of these allegations, and I was being falsely accused in a custody case, but the inmates of Greenville County didn't know that; they just knew that their new cellmate had just made the evening news.

Needless to say, just after the evening news ended, the questions began. First off, the guys started asking me about the allegation that I had molested a toddler. I told them about the four-year custody case and that the accuser was my ex-wife, which settled the issue for everyone in the room. That led to the next question of why the news reports made such a big deal about my arrest. One inmate even asked me if I was famous and if this was a political hit job. I answered no to both, but I had my doubts on the latter point.

By the third day in jail, I was getting desperate. Every day was emotionally taxing. Wakeup calls and inmate counts took place at around 6am each day after which we were served a stale breakfast of bran flakes and a hard biscuit. Then, the daily waiting game began to see if this would be the day I would be released. I filled the waiting period by reading the Bible, sometimes aloud, while some of the others listened or played checkers.

At the end of the third day behind bars, my criminal defense attorney informed me that he would be headed to a bond hearing the next morning (Friday) before the Court of General Sessions. By then, my case had become a statewide story. After the news story broke on the evening of the 15th, my production team at the radio station hosted my show in my absence and explained to the public what was going on and why this entire situation was a miscarriage of justice.

The radio listeners' show of support for me was overwhelming, not only on my show but on that of my colleague Dr. Tony Beam's morning show, "Christian Worldview Today," and even from competitor stations across the state. The public outcry against my arrest prompted the Greenville City Police spokesman to tell the press that they would not have arrested me "unless they had enough evidence to prosecute." Those words would come back to haunt him later.

This public attention put additional pressure on the district attorney's office, the Greenville City Police, and even the court presiding over the bond hearing. The result was added scrutiny of the process which we believed would lead to my bonding out of jail before the weekend. That was exactly what happened. On Friday morning, the Court of General Sessions approved a $25,000 bond amount which my family paid with a cashier's check in order to secure my release.

I called from the jail's phone to check in with my family around the time I thought the bond would be approved and was elated to learn that I was going to be released later that day. The moment I got off of the phone after learning that I would be released, I openly said, "Praise the Lord God of Israel Who has heard my cry." I think my cellmates thought I was a nut, but they at least respected me after the events of the week.

The time I was approved to be bonded out of jail to the time I was actually released was around 10 hours. I was removed from my cell and taken to be processed out on bond. This process meant signing the bond papers and having my court documents for my trial provided to me. The same officer who had taken some semblance of sympathy for me on the day of my arrest issued yet another warning. His first warning about keeping the charges to myself was pretty apt, and what he said to me on the day of my release was even more prophetic: "it's going to be a lot different for you now."

I was released just after midnight on Saturday, October 19, 2014. My mom and dad picked me up from the detention center. As I walked out the front door, that was the first time I had seen anything other than the walls of a jail cell since Tuesday afternoon. I was shaken, starving, and had lost nearly 10 pounds. But, at least, I could see the sky again. My first stop was a 24-hour McDonald's so that I could have a meal that didn't taste like it was past its expiration date.

Then, I got a midnight call from my executive producer and my lawyer who said they were still working on getting me reunited with my son and getting my name publicly cleared. Both of those objectives, which were inexorably linked, would occupy much of the next four months.

CHAPTER 14

EXONERATION

I woke up on the Saturday morning after my release, still missing my son but still with resolve to right the wrong. I was determined to win back my little boy and to have my good name restored. Friends from around the state and across the country came to my aide. Friends wrote letters to me, came to spend time with my family and me, and even helped raise some of the money I needed to clear my name and restore my custody rights with my son.

Being out of jail on bond did not mean that I was in the clear. The felony charges filed against me were still hanging over my head, and the DSS investigation was still underway. This new reality hit me hard in early November when two of my best friends got married just a few miles across the South Carolina border in Lake Lure, North Carolina, and I literally had to have written permission from the prosecutor to cross state lines to attend. This new "normal" could not be maintained; I was determined to get my son, and my reputation, back.

The DSS investigation was finally complete, and they came back with no findings against me regarding the false sexual-abuse allegations. The DSS, once again, unfounded Cassidy's allegations against me and threw out the claim that I had abused my own son. DSS, instead, decided to pursue a family-court, DSS trial as to mental endangerment to our child.

I am convinced that the DSS only filed the mental-endangerment case against both Cassidy and me in response to the public nature of the case. Media and community attention was concentrated on this case to such a degree that every agency and individual involved was looking to cover their backsides. The result was a tedious and tenuous process that took much more time than was necessary.

The DSS decided to have a trial wherein they, representing the state, would try to "convict" Cassidy and me for mental endangerment even though they unfounded all of the sexual-abuse claims against me. A three-day DSS trial was scheduled in the Greenville County Family Court with Cassidy and me as the defendants and DSS as the plaintiff. It was three days of rehashing everything that had transpired between Cassidy and me for the past four years.

Cassidy's entire defense strategy was to double down on her accusations against me. In effect, she was saying that she risked mental endangerment of our son because she was just trying to protect him from me. Even after every shred of evidence disproved her claims, and every expert examining the case agreed that the allegations were unfounded, she continued to allege that I was "a perpetrator" during the family-court proceedings. Her allegations were so outrageous all over again that I was having a hard time sitting still while she said it. At one point, one of my lawyers had to put his hand on my shoulder to sort of hold me in my seat in front of the courtroom.

At the end of the three-day DSS trial, a verdict was handed down that finally started putting an end to all of this insanity. After some deliberation, the family-court judge read his ruling to us in court. There would be no DSS finding against me. Period. Not only were there no sexual-abuse findings, there were no mental-endangerment findings.

Cassidy, on the other hand, had a DSS finding made against her for risking mental endangerment based on the allegations she made in an attempt to alienate my son from me.

My counsel and I were elated. This was the biggest step forward since the nightmare began four months earlier. Best yet, my son would be placed in the custody of my brother and sister-in-law until the criminal charges against me were formally dropped. Until then, I could visit my son at my brother's house because I had not seen him since late September. On the evening of the DSS trial ruling, I was reunited with my sweet son at my brother's house. It was one of the sweetest days of my life. I don't know who cried more, my son or me.

The DSS ruling and my reunion with my son happened on a Friday. During the week after, my counsel and I began a full-bore effort to have the ridiculous criminal charges that had been filed against me dropped. DSS had unfounded the sexual-abuse allegations weeks ago. Now, the accuser had a DSS finding against her for her role in making such outrageous claims in the first place.

On top of the case falling apart before it could ever be prosecuted, public pressure was beginning to build. The district attorney's office is in the Greenville County Courthouse downtown and is not normally the scene of many protests. As the DA's office continued to sit on my case despite the DSS's dismissal of the sexual-abuse allegations for the second time, supporters and listeners to my radio program started organizing protests.

According to a friend of mine who has practiced criminal defense law in Greenville for years, there is no precedent for a protest against the prosecutors for not dismissing a case. In our case, they had two, right there on the sidewalk. I learned of the first one while I was downtown one afternoon for a lunch meeting. A friend of mine with whom I was having lunch decided to drive me past the courthouse to see the huge crowd that had assembled and were holding signs that read, "REUNITE JOSH AND [HIS SON]." Even the local news stations had shown up and had cameras rolling so that the scene could be broadcast on the evening news.

After the DSS unfounded the sexual-abuse allegations against me, followed by the protests on the sidewalk, I was asked to provide interviews to local news outlets. My team and I took advantage of these interviews to call on the district attorney's office to drop the charges and allow my son and me to see one another again on normal terms, instead of him continuing to see me on a very limited basis.

Finally, after all of the DSS investigations, television interviews, and protests on the courthouse sidewalk, the prosecution issued a statement that they were dismissing the charges. County Solicitor (DA) Walt Wilkins issued a statement saying that the charges would be dropped due to "insufficient evidence." (We later learned from one of the deputy solicitors that the sex-crimes prosecutor had told the detective prior to my arrest that the case would not be prosecuted.) On February 21, 2015, the charges were dropped after tens of thousands in legal fees, my sweet son being sent to a foster home, and my enduring a week in jail and public humiliation.

On the evening of the charges being dismissed, I did sit-down interviews with all local news channels and vowed to use the experience to help other children and families avoid similar circumstances. I said in those interviews that we would seek to change state laws to ensure that children have both parents, even in divorce, and to prevent the criminal justice system from being used to influence family-court proceedings. This book is part of those efforts. I wrote this with the hope that other children can avoid the trauma my son endured and the stress and pain parents endure when falsely accused.

The final chapter consists of my recommendations to reform family law to protect other children and their parents.

PART 3

THE NEED FOR FAMILY LAW
REFORM IN AMERICA

CHAPTER 15

HOW TO KEEP THIS FROM HAPPENING TO ANYONE ELSE

What happened to my family and to me could happen to anyone. In the aftermath of divorce, people do things that are desperate and irrational in order to win custody disputes and the upper hand in financial matters. The current, broken family-court systems that exist in most states exacerbate the problem, taking difficult situations and making them much worse. The very structure of most states' family-law proceedings throw gasoline on the fire from the very beginning, starting with the initial temporary hearing.

A temporary hearing is the first hearing that a divorcing and/or separating couple will attend after one or both parties files for separation. In cases involving the custody of children, these temporary hearings will determine what custody of minor children and financial arrangements will be put into place during the intervening period between initial separation and the final divorce/custody order.

Though, legally speaking, these hearings are supposed to be "without prejudice"—meaning that they are not supposed to influence the final divorce/custody order—they almost always do. In states like my home state of South Carolina, the waiting period for divorce absent a qualifying reason for an expedited divorce is 12 months. In most cases, once that temporary hearing has concluded, and the temporary order is in place, it will govern the custody and financial arrangements until a final hearing/order is put into place up to a year later.

These temporary orders usually follow an 80/20 custody structure wherein one parent will have primary legal custody of the child or children and at least 80% physical custody while the other parent will become the visiting parent to their children with what is normally known as standard visitation. The visiting parent may as well be a visitor to their children as standard visitation is essentially every other weekend and one night of visitation in the off week. In about 80% of cases nationwide, the visiting parent is the father, and the primary parent is the mother due to most states' existing family-law structures.

Because of the high stakes and the short duration (average 15 minutes) of the temporary hearing, the tension is high. Lawyers and their clients come into those hearings prepared to utterly destroy their former partners in order to gain the upper hand in the divorce proceedings. As I discussed in an earlier chapter, this is exactly what happened in my case early on in my battle to be an active father to my son.

In family law, there are all kinds of legal presumptions. There are presumptions related to property rights, alimony, child support, etc. One presumption that is glaringly missing is a presumption of joint custody when a marriage or relationship dissolves. As a result, children caught in the crossfire are subjected to what is, in effect, government-mandated, single-parent childhood. We must reform our family-law codes to protect children from the fallout from failed families and not force them apart from either one of their biological parents.

Much of the drama and pain associated with divorces and custody battles stems from a lack of this joint-custody presumption in most states' family law codes. As famed family lawyer and CNN contributor Fred Silberberg wrote in an article for *Huffington Post* in June 2012,

> Each year, cases are tied up in court by one parent trying to maintain control over the custody of the children. In these situations, the parent who is seeking equal custody can be tied up in very expensive litigation to establish a right to their children that, had the parents not been divorced, they would automatically have.

The cost of no equal-parenting provisions is staggering on both economic and emotional terms as parents engage in a legal battle with one another to win the custody prize.

For this reason, I have advocated for shared parenting reforms since 2012 when the issue came before the South Carolina Legislature. My conviction that these common-sense reforms would lead to many more-amicable outcomes has only grown over the four years since. My own personal story is a testament to this truth as the bitter battle that put my son in foster care and me in a jail cell began with a venomous temporary-custody hearing in 2011. A presumption of equal-parenting protects the parental rights of both parents that they would automatically have if they were not separating or divorcing as well as ensures that children have a healthy relationship with both parents.

If we made a presumption of joint legal and physical custody a matter of statutory law, it would have numerous and immediate positive effects. First, it would remove the incentive for two warring parties to go nuclear in temporary hearings, thus making their irreconcilable differences that much greater. The presumption that they will be co-parenting their children will remove some of the incentive for them to engage in costly and rancorous litigation that makes them even less likely to keep their children from the crossfire. It also will prevent parents from litigating their former spouse or partner for no other reason than increasing their child-support remunerations, thus using their children as leverage for greater financial gain. Both of these changes will benefit already-back-logged family courts that are so congested with these frivolous cases that they cannot hear new cases or urgent cases in which there is actual abuse or neglect.

Presumption of joint custody will fundamentally transform family law in the United States and will send a message to society that we believe in the critical importance having both an active mother and father in the lives of their children. Fostering environments in which former spouses and partners have to lay aside their personal animosities for the sake of their shared children is enormously beneficial for society as it will contribute to less family litigation, stronger social structures for millions of children caught in the tragedy of divorce, and will lead to a reduction in criminal domestic violence and abuse among warring parents. The social benefits are innumerable.

As we discussed in earlier chapters, research shows that children with active, two-parent childhoods do better in school, are less likely to live at or below the poverty line, are less likely to abuse drugs and alcohol, are less likely to commit suicide in adolescence and teenage years, and are less likely to be incarcerated as adults. For these reasons alone, it behooves us to espouse public policy that places a premium on two active and engaged parents for all children.

There are powerful special interests that oppose these common-sense reforms, largely out of parochial self-interest. Here in South Carolina, there has been no greater opponent than the South Carolina Bar Association, which views such reforms as a threat to what is nationally a $50 billion per year industry. The interests of parents and children and the interests of bar associations across the country are at odds. The public must take the side of parents and children, not that of the lawyers hoping to cash in.

Think about what $50 billion that is currently spent on family-law litigation every year would mean for children in this country. That would be $50 billion more per year going toward children's college funds, extracurricular activities, educational achievement, medical needs, dental visits, and overall well-being. It would mean fewer children living at or below the poverty line because their parents are engaged in a never-ending cycle of custody litigation.

These reforms are achievable because they have already been passed in states' legislatures in Florida and Minnesota and have been introduced in legislatures in Connecticut, Tennessee, South Carolina, Texas, and in many other states. The laws being considered in these states are all very similar; they provide for a presumption of joint legal and physical custody unless there is demonstrable proof of actual child abuse, substance abuse, neglect, or abandonment on the part of one of more parents. These reforms would ensure that, just because a marriage or relationship ends, the children from that relationship will not be relegated to a semi-orphanage.

I wholeheartedly support family-law reforms that put parents back in charge of the lives of their children rather than government agencies. Current custody laws give too much power to family courts and social-services agencies concerning the rearing of children. In the process of deciding disputes between two warring parents, the state weighs in on a child's diet, religious instruction, educational arrangements, and recreational activities. This is unacceptable, and it represents one of the greatest overreaches of government in modern American history. Fair and equitable family-law reforms would put parents back in the driver's seat with regard to the rearing of their children and will force adults to act like grown-ups for the sakes of their minor children.

I believe in family-law reform that is equitable for both moms and dads. My support for shared parenting is not about punishing mothers; instead, it is about protecting both parents and, above all, their children. Some so-called fathers' rights advocates have taken on the cause of family-law reform as a means of exacting vengeance on their former spouses or women in general for the pain they have experienced. This is not my motivation. I don't believe for a minute that family-law reform ought to be pursued to punish moms or to impugn the heroism of single mothers who are struggling to provide for their children in the absence of an engaged father. The reforms that I am advocating would equally benefit both mothers and fathers.

According to most model shared-parenting legislation I have read, shared parenting requires shared responsibility. Gone are the days when deadbeat parents left the other hanging to pay all of the expenses of raising a child alone. Under draft legislation, any parent who does not pay his or her fair share of the bills agreed upon in the custody order forfeits the presumption of joint custody and the equal time that it provides. Statistics indicate that the closer a custody arrangement is to shared, physical custody, the higher the compliance rates regarding child support. This makes sense that parents who spend more quality time with their children feel more invested in them and are much more supportive, financially and otherwise.

These statutory guidelines would ensure that two parents remain involved in their child's life and that they act more in the interests of their children than out of their anger toward one another. Cases like mine would be much less frequent as years of seething resentment and competing interests will not build to the point of exploding into a criminal case because of an unresolved custody dispute.

Preventing nightmares like the one my son and I endured should be one of the chief goals of family-law reform. These reforms, coupled with changes to criminal procedure associated with custody cases, can help to prevent a parent from being prosecuted for just trying to be a parent. I was blessed to be a public person at the time of being falsely accused because so many people came to my aide and helped me overcome the injustice. I was provided the means and the public relations to prove my innocence and restore my good name. Too many fathers don't have that support.

Imagine if what happened to me had happened to a 24-year-old manager at McDonald's who is falsely accused of molesting his own son by the child's mother. With no public profile to build support and no way to spend the tens of thousands of dollars necessary to fight back, he would likely face conviction for a crime he did not commit. I know this is true because I have witnessed it firsthand. I was arrested for no reason, without any evidence to back up my former wife's allegations. If it were not for the support I received from so many, I would have sat in jail for at least a year awaiting trial, and my son would have sat in a foster home until the issue was resolved.

In addition to reforming the family-court system, states need to put into place safeguards on criminal procedure. If there is a known custody battle that has preceded an allegation, there needs to be extra care taken. Instead of merely having a magistrate court—which does not handle criminal proceedings—sign off on a class-A felony warrant as occurred in my case, those warrants need to be reviewed and decided by either a district attorney or criminal-court judge. It's unconscionable that a warrant can be taken out against one parent who is accused of abuse by another parent in a custody battle that is signed by a magistrate with no authority to hear a criminal case.

Finally, states should enforce perjury laws in family-court cases. A friend of mine who has practiced family law in South Carolina for over 30 years recently told me that he has never once seen a parent prosecuted for perjury in a family-court case, even when it was abundantly clear that a person intentionally lied under oath. If parents who knowingly lied in family court were prosecuted for perjury like people are in criminal court, most of the allegations made in temporary hearings and custody trials would cease almost immediately.

Family-law reform is essential if we hope to regain any sort of sanity in custody disputes. Reasonable reform would go a long way toward incentivizing two parents who have decided that they don't like one another anymore to care about their children more than they hate their former partner. Family courts should, above all, protect children by protecting the role played by both parents in their lives.

My hope is that the story I have shared in this book and the recommendations I have made regarding family-law reform will help others to avoid what my family and I have endured. It is my hope that we will restore respect for the role of both mothers and fathers and that no father like me will ever again be put on trial for wanting nothing more than to be a dad who is engaged in the life of his child.

DON'T BE NEXT

I wrote this book out of the deep conviction that I was put through my trial to save others from the same agony. In the first book of the Bible, *Genesis*, there is a story of a young man named Joseph who had a great dream at an early age. Joseph, a forefather of the Jewish people and the Jewish and Christian faiths, dreamt as a teenager that he would be called upon to lead his people, something that generated resentment in the hearts of his brothers. As a result, the young dreamer was sold into slavery by his own siblings and shipped off to Egypt in chains. In Egypt, he was sold to a man named Potiphar, who was essentially the ancient-Egyptian equivalent of a secretary of defense. The young dreamer was then accused, falsely, of trying to sleep with Potiphar's wife after she tried to seduce him though he fled, which landed him in prison. Over the course of 13 years, from the time Joseph was 17 until he was 30, he endured hardship, false accusation, and, ultimately, false imprisonment.

Through all of these trials, Joseph's faithfulness to God remained steadfast. Despite his circumstances, Joseph still retained confidence that God had called him to lead his people and that God was, indeed, good. Through a myriad of providentially-orchestrated circumstances, Joseph was promoted from inmate to in-charge—literally, overnight. Because of his faithfulness to his God, Joseph gained favor with God and with men and, at just the right moment, the Pharaoh of Egypt made him vice regent, second-in-command. He went from prisoner to the pinnacle of power so that the pain that had been sown in his own life could be used to save the lives of many people who would suffer under famine if Joseph had not been elevated to power at just the right moment.

I assure you that I do not see myself as the equivalent of Joseph, nor do I have designs to be vice regent of anything. I do, however, believe that—like Joseph—God allowed me to endure the trial that I did so that I could be an advocate for reform. I do believe that, like Joseph, the Lord allowed me to go to jail so that I might be used to save others from a similar fate. What happened to me was truly unbelievable. To this day, I still have a difficult time accepting that what happened to my son and to me could ever happen in the United States of America… much less in a conservative state like South Carolina and in the tight-knit community of Greenville that I know so very well.

After the charges against me were dropped, and I was able to begin telling my story in media interviews and newspaper articles, the most common question asked of me was, "How could this happen?" One of my very closest friends with whom I have worked in politics and talk radio for over a decade told me that he was "deeply shaken" by my arrest. He said that, if a man like me who never had so much as a speeding ticket on his criminal record, could be picked up and locked up without any evidence, no one was safe from a similar scenario. I would love to tell him that he is wrong, but the truth is that he hit the nail on the head. Our family and criminal-court systems do not have in place sufficient safeguards to protect parents from false allegations that could even lead to their arrest and imprisonment.

Since charges were dropped against me in February of 2015, I have received a veritable deluge of emails, letters, direct messages on Facebook, and calls at my office from parents in similar situations. It has become abundantly clear to me that mine was, while certainly much more public than most, just one of many stories of failed marriages that had devolved into bitter custody cases that became criminal proceedings. The sheer number of people from whom I have heard is staggering. I am saddened to learn that my case is not as rare as it should be.

The scenario that keeps me up at night is that false allegations like those that were leveled at me are leveled against a young father working as a shift manager at Chick-Fil-A, who has neither the public profile nor the resources to fight back. If not for the grace of God in my life and the public support that rallied to my side, I might still be sitting in a jail cell today, awaiting trial for something that I not only never did but of which I could never conceive. The public perceives that it is very difficult to be falsely arrested because "probable cause" for an arrest warrant is difficult to obtain. Not true. Unfortunately, the threshold for a warrant to be issued for your arrest is much lower than you could imagine, and if you're in a particularly nasty custody case, it is highly possible that you could be arrested on the word of your former spouse or partner.

In addition to the family-law reform recommendations I laid out in the prior chapter, states need to reconsider their criminal-law codes when it comes to custody cases. There should be a legal requirement for family courts and criminal courts to share records and proceedings. That bitter custody cases can end up as criminal prosecutions is unconscionable. The prospect of being prosecuted by a bitter co-parent is a strong deterrent to two parents staying involved in the lives of their shared children. This is a shame that could be easily remedied by some simple reforms that could prevent such catastrophes.

Legislatures should enact laws that prevent criminal charges from being pressed against accused parents, particularly when accused by the other parent in a nasty custody case, until after a social-services investigation can be completed. It is detrimentally expensive both to the defendant and to the state for parallel cases over the same allegations to proceed in two separate court systems. As in my case, I had to defend myself in a family-court action involving the DSS as well as in the Court of General Sessions (criminal court). This required me to hire a total of three attorneys as well as to pay court costs in both systems. Even after the social-services investigation had cleared me of any wrongdoing, I still had to wait several months for the criminal charges against me to be dismissed even though the same allegations and evidence were involved.

Reforming state laws to ensure that family-court and social-services investigations are completed before criminal charges are brought against accused parents would save much misery for families and much money for state agencies. Such reforms would also save falsely-accused persons the incredible embarrassment and pain of being arrested and publically scorned for an alleged crime that he or she never committed. Once an arrest is made, a mugshot is taken, and a press statement is released, it is really hard to put the genie back into the bottle. Even for a public person like me, it has taken well over a year to tell my side of the story enough times that it has drowned out the allegations in the media. Imagine how long it would take a non-public person who does not have an hour a day on the radio and the ability to connect with the press to clear his or her name. The answer: his or her entire lifetime.

The crisis in our nation's family courts has spilled over to corrupt the integrity of our criminal-justice system. This unholy alliance between a failed family-court system and insufficient safeguards in the criminal-justice system with regard to allegations made during custody proceedings have further poisoned the family culture of our country. The consequences are more childhood alienation from one or more biological parents and a lifetime of pain and emotional suffering for the children caught in the crossfire. Crucial reforms must be enacted soon to save more parents and children from the pain of prison and foster care when custody cases go criminal.

Just as Joseph's suffering was used by God to save others from even greater pain, it is my prayer that the awful pain that my son and I have endured will help other families avoid even greater challenges. I hope that this book will help jumpstart a national conversation about the need to reform outdated family-law codes, make critical criminal-justice reforms, and foster a culture of two-parent childhood for children—even in the age of a 55% divorce rate. Joseph's seeming defeat was his and his country's triumph. I hope that my darkest hour will save many mothers, fathers, and children from enduring theirs.

ABOUT THE AUTHOR

Josh Kimbrell is the host of "Common Cents w/ Josh Kimbrell," a daily conservative talk radio program focused on South Carolina public policy issues that broadcasts out of Greenville, South Carolina. In addition to his work on the radio, Kimbrell chairs the Palmetto Conservative Alliance, which is a public policy advocacy organization in South Carolina that promotes pro free-market principles, pro-life, and pro-family policies in the State. Kimbrell also serves on numerous boards for military veterans' issues and Christian business advocacy. Kimbrell and his son reside in Spartanburg, South Carolina.

More information about Kimbrell and his public policy efforts may be found at **www.JoshKimbrell.com**.

CPSIA information can be obtained at www.ICGtesting.com
Printed in the USA
LVOW11s0034090616

491677LV00002B/2/P